Burton, Mrs. Harrison

The merry Maid of Arcady, his Lordship, and other Stories

Burton, Mrs. Harrison

The merry Maid of Arcady, his Lordship, and other Stories

ISBN/EAN: 9783743336773

Manufactured in Europe, USA, Canada, Australia, Japa

Cover: Foto ©ninafisch / pixelio.de

Manufactured and distributed by brebook publishing software (www.brebook.com)

Burton, Mrs. Harrison

The merry Maid of Arcady, his Lordship, and other Stories

Contents

	Page
The Merry Maid of Arcady	1
Worrosquoyacke	51
Leaves from the Diary of Ruth Marchmont, Spinster	117
Thirteen at Table	165
At a Winter House-Party	197
The Secret of San Juan	223
"The Stranger Within Thy Gate"	279
His Lordship	301

List of Illustrations

                                          Page

At the Horse Show . . . *Frontispiece*

"Wilcox did not move a muscle, but smoked his cigar in silence to the end" 80

The Holiday Dance at Worrosquoyacke   113

For permission to reproduce the original illustrations by W. T. Smedley, the Publishers are indebted to *The Ladies' Home Journal.*

The Merry Maid of Arcady

The Merry Maid of Arcady

MISS POINTDEXTER sat in her hall bedroom in the fourth story of Mrs. Penfold's boarding-house, and looked down upon the street. Her throne was a Vienna bent-wood chair, with aggressive rockers, which she had come to regard as a very nestling-place of comfort, in contrast with the only other chair the room contained — a hard wooden monster of the variety appertaining to suites displayed by emporiums that fit out the sidewalks with their wares, under the label "Chaste and Cheap."

Recently, since Miss Pointdexter had resided, summer and winter, with Mrs. Penfold for ten years, the boarding-house keeper had, in a burst of generosity, furnished her room with one of those sets in highly polished ash, going so far as to substitute for the wooden bedstead one in iron, painted white, with brass knobs and rails.

The Merry Maid of Arcady

From the date of this addition to her kingdom Miss Pointdexter had felt the same fluttering complacency that animated her school friend Mrs. Algernon Thorne, of Madison Avenue, when that lady's husband consented to buy the house adjoining their family mansion, throw the two into one, and make over the whole in the best style of the American Renaissance in art.

The substitution of an iron bedstead for the wooden one had not only added full three inches in breadth to Miss Pointdexter's domain, but had imparted to it a note of decoration, of coquetry, of living up to date and fashion, that refreshed agreeably the jaded spirit of the beneficiary. Last, but far from least in the list of Mrs. Penfold's concessions to the promptings of conscience, had been the new papering of Miss Pointdexter's walls, with a paper at thirty cents the roll, which, it must be admitted, was five cents more than the most grasping imagination of a boarder could have demanded. Miss Pointdexter never knew that her allowance of wallpaper was left over from a first-floor bedroom. To her dying day she cherished the illusion that it was a spontaneous efflorescence of Mrs. Penfold's humanity to a sister long in distress through an environment of chocolate-colored stripes dotted with bunches of pea-green grapes.

The new decoration of her walls revealed to Miss Pointdexter's ravished eyes a pattern of honeysuckles, yellow and coral, on a pale yellow ground. This harmonizing sufficiently with the rather threadbare brown carpet, Miss Pointdexter was fired with ambition to curtain her window. For this purpose she made several furtive visits to the large shops that advertise bargains in such stuffs as she desired. But when one set of lace curtains after another, at seventy-five cents the pair, had been begrudgingly unfolded to her gaze, she came away from them disconsolate. No æsthetic pleasure was possible to be derived from these great sprawling designs of roses and dahlias upon a coarse Nottingham foundation. And the better grades of patterns, the spots and stars and trefoils, must remain upon their shelves out of reach of her little hand and purse.

Although Miss Pointdexter had so long

The Merry Maid of Arcady

been a dweller in the honeycomb of Mrs. Penfold's two houses filled with boarders, she had been born to a more liberal horizon. In the household out of which she came, one of the sayings impressed upon young people was, that whatever Providence ordained for them, whether good fortune or reverse, it should be accepted quietly, not carrying one's affairs to other ears (unless the confidence were sought by those who had a right to know). Miss Pointdexter was no longer a young person, but she often found herself recalling these utterances of dead lips as reverently and simply as she had first received them long years ago, just as, quite unconsciously, when at night she had screwed her fringe of front hair into chrysalids of curls for the morrow, she knelt down by the iron bedstead with brass rails and prayed God to make her a "good girl."

The Pointdexter tradition of silent endurance was, however, infringed upon by its inheritor when Mrs. Berry, the laundress, instead of sending her boy, as usual, with Miss Pointdexter's wash, condescended to mount the third flight of stairs and interpose her own ample person into the space between bed and wall, crushing the rightful occupant into the window.

"Well, I want to know!" Mrs. Berry had remarked, pantingly, placing the palms of her hands, corrugated by repeated immersion into soapsuds, upon her matronly hips; "if this ain't real handsome! It reminds me of one of the bedrooms at Mis' Hall's when I wet-nussed her eldest, the same as was stroke oar at Harvard last year, Miss Pointdexter, and as fine a young man as you'd wish to see; an' did you read about the deebutt of her youngest girl, ma'am, in the *Evening World* o' yesterday? They're real folks, I call 'em; think nuthin' o' spendin' five hundred dollars fur a curtain made o' 'Merican Beauty roses to hang between the foldin'-doors — an' that's the kind o' place I'd be in now if I hadn't listened to Berry, an' set up fur ourselves, an' he takin' to bad habits, or he might 'a' stayed coachman to the Four Hundred, i'stead o' lyin' abed in the room over the laundry, an' thumpin' an' bellowin' fur me to come an' wait on him, an' me workin' fur the six of us."

"I wish I had a curtain worth a dollar and fifty cents," said Miss Pointdexter, as she counted out the small sum accruing to Mrs. Berry into that lady's hand. Directly after having given expression to this aspiration, Virginia felt a flush run up into the roots of her hair. What would the Pointdexter shades say to this revelation of her poverty and unsatisfied yearning, and before a washer-woman, too?

Luckily Mrs. Berry, accustomed to look at such things in the concrete, missed the fine point of Miss Pointdexter's offence against family dicta. Entering into the spirit of the occasion, she declared heartily that it would be a shame to let the room go without the finishing touch of drapery, and proffered to her client the gift of a suddenly remembered pair of dotted muslin curtains with goffered frills, that she had "done up" for a lady who went away to Europe without leaving an address, and had never been heard from since.

"If you think, Mrs. Berry," Miss Pointdexter said, slowly, her brain whirling with the double excitement of the offer and her doubt as to the moral responsibility involved, "that I would do no harm to the curtains by using them — luckily there is a pole and rings — and you would let me pay you what I can afford toward them, with the understanding that if the lady ever comes back you will let me know at once, and that I will then meet the expense of doing them up again"— here she paused, revolving the prudence of this outlay — "I should be most glad, most thankful" — this, again, stuck like a bur in the poor gentlewoman's throat, and was bravely cleared away — "*most* thankful," she repeated, in a firm voice.

The Merry Maid of Arcady

"Law bless your soul, Miss Pointdexter, you nor me ain't never goin' to hear o' that owner again. I can't use 'em, an' there they've been lying by and turnin' yellow these two years, so I guess I'll just have to run 'em through the wash again, anyhow."

"Oh, no!" said Virginia, suavely. She knew she could not afford to have them done up *now*. "A slight tinge of écru is really more fashionable than white, Mrs. Berry."

In the watches of the night she awoke

to confront this insincerity, and to repent it. But by the next day, when the curtains arrived and were put up by Miss Pointdexter, standing on the top of her chest of drawers, her prickings of conscience made themselves conspicuously less felt. By the time she had scrambled down, pushed the chest of drawers back into its place, and tied the curtains on either side with yellow bows, Miss Pointdexter's moral hardening was accomplished. She almost danced for joy. Diving down to the bottom of a trunk of relics kept under her bed, she fished out of its faintly musty interior one or two belongings of her father — killed on the Confederate side at Appomattox Court House — and turned them over, wondering if she could bring herself to cancel her debt of gratitude to Mrs. Berry by devoting one of these to that lady's suffering liege. There was among them a gray flannel shirt, made by Virginia's mother to put in the kit of her husband when departing for the war whence he returned nevermore. It had been worn in camp and in battle, and now lay stiffened in the folds of a quarter of a century. When Miss Pointdexter took it out of the chest, under the light of her single gas burner, she gave the quick gasp that never failed to follow the touch of its soft old texture.

The Merry Maid of Arcady

"What it means, who remembers? who cares now?" she said to herself. "Only a few like me here, and in the South thousands that are carrying it to their graves. Soon I may be gone, and when strange hands turn over my things, I couldn't bear to have this held up for laughter because it was kept in the trunk of an old maid. Better part with it now, and little by little I'll find something to do with the rest."

Thus Mr. Berry came into possession of the Confederate flannel shirt, which, to his wife's satisfaction, he took into immediate wear — dying in it, to her equal relief, a month or two later in that same season.

Miss Pointdexter's room was warmed by leaving the door open for the furnace heat of the halls to come in. This method, shared by a young Southerner who occupied the larger room adjoining, brought the two into an acquaintance that had proved an era in her life. Miss Pointdexter had been known by old boarders to speak of an absent nephew. But he had died in California many years before, and now she spoke of nobody belonging to her to anybody in the house.

When he was away, she would often go into young Alexander's room and tidy his table, rummaging in his drawers for socks with holes and shirts with broken buttonholes, which she would mend and restore unknown to the innocent youth, who declared his chambermaid to be a trump.

Always exquisitely neat in person, Miss Virginia's pale cameo face, with the fine brown hair cut and frizzed above the low brow, the large mild gray eyes, and the mouth that was still a Cupid's bow, often caught the attention of strangers, who would say, "That must have been a pretty woman in her day." But to young Alexander only did her face break into the luminous smile that convinced him she was still more than pretty. He found out that she could laugh, too — laugh with the sudden ringing joy of a school-girl. But that was seldom.

Young Alexander had fallen into the habit of stopping after dinner in the boarding-house parlor to exchange a few words with her; then to tell her of his business and its prospects of advance; then of his increasing social opportunities and introductions to people who made society; finally of his home, his mother and sisters in Carolina. In all of which she sympathized in a manner unusual to her quiet self.

The Merry Maid of Arcady

On the evening when Miss Pointdexter sat down in her completely renovated room ("for who would be apt to look down at the carpet," she argued, "on coming in to face such a wall-paper and curtains?") she had turned down the gas, and seated herself in the Vienna bent-wood rocking-chair to look out of the window into the street. For some time past her eyes had given her warning they would no longer be trifled with by a single "fish-tail" burner fixed at some distance above them, when she sat under it to read or write or sew. A visit to the oculist, so much a matter of course to the well-to-do, was not considered by her. A drop-light and

The Merry Maid of Arcady

Argand burner, or, what seemed the pitch of luxury, a student's lamp, would cost her a week's board. So she often sat now in the dark in preference to the boarding-house parlor below. And so sitting, she thought of many things not cheerful.

On the tiny table, squeezed into the recess of the door leading into the adjoining room, lay a new novel lent her by young Alexander that morning — a book read of, heard of, long coveted, the perusal of which would have made her dull evening more eventful and stirring than one spent at dinner and theatre or ball by the sated souls whose carriages rolled continually in her sight up and down the long avenue coated with light snow.

It did not occur to Virginia to begrudge these people their privileges, for she was one of the rare beings " with whom the melodies abide of the everlasting chime." She was well balanced, cheerful by nature, and to-night, especially, she " carried music in her heart " in the consciousness of surroundings that satisfied her æsthetic craving in a fashion consolatory for most other earthly woes. For she was all a woman in this respect, a commonplace woman who likes prettiness and millinery effects. Could she have chosen the vocation that was to eke out her little patrimony into a support in the metropolis, her lot might have been cast in one of those bowers of tinsel beauty where soft-voiced gentlewomen who have seen better days take counsel with their customers about lamp shades, sofa cushions, and favors for the cotillon, or else in an emporium of decorative art, where she could have had the daily solace of handling frost-work embroideries, and linens reft of their threads to be wrought into fine silken spider-webs. Miss Pointdexter sighed now and then in gentle envy of those women she knew who could paint the bloated Cupids, Strephons, and Chloes that are seen breaking out in pink, like erysipelas, on a background of ribbed canvas. This seemed to her something one should be born to achieve. On the Pointdexter plantation, on the Eastern Shore of Maryland, cutting out garments of cotton domestic for the colored people, and pickling and preserving, had been esteemed a more important part of woman's whole duty than the culture of brush and pigment in decoration of unoffending surfaces.

As it was, Virginia had to spend her days in the prosaic atmosphere of an industry established by a blooming young woman of good society for the aid of her less fortunate sisters. Here she "took in" the plain work sewed at the homes of the workers, and "gave out" the elementary portions of brides' and babies' wardrobes. Sometimes her thirst for pretty things was stayed by the handling of inconceivably fine linen and flannel stuffs, with thread lace for trimming, which she well knew how to appreciate, since no Pointdexter girl was allowed to "come out" into society without a dozen of what the Vicar of Wakefield's ladies would have tranquilly called "shifts," every stitch set by hand, and all garnished with hemstitched ruffles of linen cambric and real Valenciennes.

But, for the most part, Virginia's days were dull, her associates poorer and with less opportunity for indulgence of taste than herself. She often went for so many hours without smiling that she forgot she had once been called, after the florid fashion of Southern admirers of the belles whom they delight to honor, "The Merry Maid of Arcady."

The Merry Maid of Arcady

Arcady was the style and title in former days of the Pointdexter plantation, sold to pay its debts to a prosperous Northern man, who had "restored" it, and changed the name to Belleville; and the feet of the Merry Maid never wandered in that direction now. These things trooped through her mind as she sat in the dark, wishing that she could read young Alexander's book, and chiding herself for wanting anything when her cup was that day so unusually full. A streak of light from the hall fell through the door agape across her wall, and from time to time she looked complacently at her honeysuckles, and thought how well their colors came out. And then Memory, the wizard, carried her back to a certain day when she had sat in an arbor and watched a branch of living honeysuckle sway in the wind of a summer's morning, and parted with the man who had been her promised husband, because she saw that he had gone over to her best friend. Coral honeysuckle and yellow "custard" honeysuckle mingled upon that arbor, built in the shape of a little kiosk, and an established place for flirtations and the like in the annals of Arcady plantation. The crisp clean-cut trumpets of the "coral" stood out against a blue Maryland sky as she looked now, and she could smell the rich breath of the "custard." What's more, she could see the peculiar iris of the young man's eye as he gravely accepted her dismissal, believing it to be the freak of a spoiled beauty, and questioning her with a full and honest gaze that withdrew unsatisfied by fact.

Virginia had been right. The heart that had wavered away from her soon passed into the keeping of another, and Mr. and Mrs. Algernon Thorne had for years lived and flourished among the elect of society in the great metropolis that also sheltered, not far away from their stately dwelling, the friend of their early youth. Soon after Miss Pointdexter's arrival to try her fortune in New York she had presented herself one morning at the portal of Mrs.

Thorne's still unregenerate but sufficiently imposing town house. Recalling the weeks spent by Alida Nesbitt as the guest of Arcady — where she had first arrived a meagre and ill-cared-for school-girl, brought home for the holidays by the generous Virginia to save her from the dulness of life in a dull town under a dull step-mother's control, to come and come again every summer, till, as a pretty graduate of eighteen, she witched away Virginia's lover — it seemed to Miss Pointdexter's simple soul that it was very meet and right for her to make a first call on Mrs. Thorne.

As she had stood wiping her little boots on the Thorne door-mat, Virginia had a curious recollection of once giving the slippers from her own feet that Alida might match a costume and dance in them at a ball. She had often supplemented Alida's scanty wardrobe with gifts from her own, then bounteously supplied with lawn and organdies and tarlatans, when the two were going together upon the round of entertainments of which Arcady in summer was the centre. Virginia even remembered stopping at home from a delightful excursion on horseback, when Algy Thorne was to ride at her bridle rein, to lend her habit to Alida, who had arrived at Arcady without one.

How droll and far away those days seemed now; and what fun she and Alida would have in reviving their host of memories of happy girlhood! Virginia's heart warmed at these thoughts, which seemed to lift her out of the sordid present back into a time that was the crowning-point of her life's gayety and importance. How could she realize that Mrs. Algy had long since passed from the realm of such homely doings, had put behind her poverty, makeshifts, superfluous recollections, and acquaintances?

At any rate, when Virginia rang Alida's door-bell, first, it was to receive on the threshold a woeful check. The smug footman in his striped canary waistcoat and Burgundy coat and trousers looked at her once, twice, and said he rather thought Mrs. Thorne was "not at 'ome." Virginia, to whom servants were still incidentals, courteously proffered her card, and asked if he would go and see. Whereupon the

Burgundy-colored one allowed himself the double impertinence of reading her name and surveying her person, then, comparing notes over his shoulder with an authority in the background, reasserted the announcement, "Not at 'ome."

Virginia went down the high flight of stone steps chilled and mortified in spite of her better judgment. By the time she had reached the street corner she was ashamed of her own annoyance. When she got into a street car to go to her then distant lodging-place, she had cheered herself with the thought that Alida would find her card, would exclaim in sorrow at having missed her — near lunch-time, too, when it would have been so nice to keep Virginia, and have a talk about old times — and would at once write or call.

Poor Virginia! She even thought that Mrs. Thorne would call that afternoon; and remained in, ready to receive her friend in the boarding-house parlor, hoping that the old lady who made such queer noises in her throat would keep away from it, for once.

Mrs. Thorne did not call that afternoon, or any afternoon. Nor did she write.

The Merry Maid of Arcady

True, Virginia's card was found by her when looking over the contents of an India china bowl in search of the address of a man whom she desired to invite, to fill up a vacated place at one of her dinners. (You will at once judge that this was not one of her familiars whom Mrs. Thorne sought in the India china bowl, but a new man, remembered as talking rather well, who might be depended on not to have too many engagements to prevent his coming when summoned late.) How long the card of her early friend had been there Mrs. Thorne had no idea. It had a thumb-mark in one corner, for even the Burgundy-colored ones are not always immaculate at their extremities. It was made of thinnish pasteboard, and was engraved in a script of forgotten date, as follows:

Miss Pointdexter

Maryland

Over the "Maryland" was pencilled, in Virginia's well-remembered handwriting, the New York address. As Mrs. Thorne read it a surge of recollections swept over her too. The skim of thin ice that Time lays over those emotions we once thought flowers of immortality was for a moment broken. With the poor little shabby card in her hand, and a kind impulse in her heart, she went into her drawing-room to meet some ladies who had come to discuss with her the management of an Assembly they were all to matronize. The card was put down, mislaid, forgotten, remembered again next day, sought, and not found, with almost a feeling of relief that the matter was thus taken out of her hands by accident. In plain fact, Mrs. Thorne asked herself what could she do with Jinny Pointdexter without disillusioning her and wounding her? No doubt the visit had been made long before, and Jinny had left town. At Christmas Mrs. Thorne would buy something really good and pretty, and send it to the last address she had had of Jinny's in the South. But illness came to the house at Christmas, and this good intention, too, went to join the throng of the unfulfilled, and after that, Mrs. Thorne was ashamed, and did nothing at all.

The Merry Maid of Arcady

Once or twice, sitting opposite her lord at table, Mrs. Thorne had begun to pave the way to announcing to him the incident which she well knew would annoy him thoroughly, and, like the good wife she was, quailed before the idea of spoiling his after-dinner hour, and bringing his displeasure upon herself. So she never got farther than saying, "Of course you remember Virginia Pointdexter." And he had answered: "I should think I *do* remember my old sweetheart. What was it they called her down there on the Eastern Shore —'The Merry Maid of Arcady'? And what have you heard of Miss Jinny lately? Well, I hope! A pity she never married, isn't it?" At this point, Mr. Thorne's eye detected a mote in his glass of claret, he had called back the butler to ask if this were surely the Clos Vougeot, and the disclosure of a calamity in the wine-cellar had relegated the old sweetheart to her former land of shades.

Virginia, ten years after these events, had ceased to feel the sting of the earlier sense of neglect from her old friends. Something had happened, she argued, meekly; no doubt Alida had never heard *The* of her call; but still she could not bend *Merry* the Pointdexter pride to the business of *Maid of* making a new advance. She, like Mrs. *Arcady* Berry, read in the newspapers of the fine doings of her former associates. There were sons grown and at the university, and a young girl about to make her first appearance in society.

"The Merry Maid," as she sat gazing out into the night, wondered if one of these carriages rolling up the snow-covered asphalt might not contain her quondam friends returning from a dinner. She fancied Alida nestling up to Algy inside of it, and talking to him of the beauty, the accomplishments, the prospects, of their intending débutante. She wondered what it would be to feel that exquisite throbbing of mother's pride in a young blossom put forth from the parental tree — a fair round creature, of soft hues, with no lines upon her face, no furrows in her soul. Involuntarily she laid her hand on her own heart, as if to still its beatings — for these unseen scions of Algy and Alida had become her dream-children, her romance.

The Merry Maid of Arcady

Until young Alexander came into her life her fancy had fed itself with the doings of the Thorne boys and girls in most proprietary fashion, and to the exclusion of all other young people.

Young Alexander, charging with the full vigor of two-and-twenty up the third flight of Mrs. Penfold's stairs at half-past ten o'clock P.M., saw the light coming out of Miss Virginia's room, and the lone figure sitting wrapped in a shawl in the window. Quietly she came out to meet him, traces of unwonted excitement visible in her face. Under the hall gas he thought he had never seen the "old lady" look so bright and comely.

"I would not go to bed till I'd shown it to you," she said, leading him to the door of her little kingdom.

"And I was hoping you'd be up to get these while they are fresh," he answered, putting into her hand his button-hole posy of double white violets, still deliciously crisp and fragrant, which she received with pathetic rapture.

"Oh, my dear boy, how could you know there's nothing I love better than white violets!" she exclaimed, softly, although there was upon that floor nobody to disturb. The old gentleman who had the back room snored, and was then snoring like a trooper, and the lady's-maid of the first-floor lodger in the back hall bedroom slept far too well, as her mistress had had occasion to remark.

"I put it in my overcoat when I left the house where I was dining," he said, "and the fresh air brought them out. I thought of you when I found it by my plate. By-the-way, Miss Pointdexter, you ought to know these people I've been with to-night. All you Virginians and Marylanders know one another—"

"As well say that all Chinese and Japanese know one another," she answered. "Who are they?"

"The Algernon Thornes, who live a couple of blocks up the avenue from here. One of the 'successful' Southerners who came to New York just after the war. Old friends of my father's, but I never met them till the other day. This was one of Mrs. Thorne's little dinners, not her grand affairs, and I sat at table next to the girl who is to make a first appearance a fortnight hence."

"Oh, I'm so glad you've met her!" cried Miss Pointdexter, breathlessly.

"You do know them then? That's good, because it won't bore you so much for me to talk to you about them. You know I've told you about this girl and the other that I've met; but this time it's all up with me. I'm gone."

"*Isn't* she lovely?" said Miss Pointdexter, exultingly.

"Lovely is no word for it," said young Alexander, his eyes shining with fun and earnest.

"To-morrow you shall tell me everything you will," said Miss Pointdexter, giving him a glimpse of her new furnishings to end the colloquy.

"I like their calling her Champe. The way Virginians use surnames for girls is sometimes ridiculous, but this time just right."

"Champe, is it?" queried Miss Pointdexter.

"Yes; didn't you know, or is it something recent their using her middle name?"

"Marian Champe was his mother's name," answered Miss Pointdexter, dreamily; "a famous beauty of the lower James. I remember her portrait; a long neck like a swan, a blue low-cut gown, pearls of course, and one brown curl escaping behind the ear, with brown eyes and arched eyebrows."

"Why, you must be a witch," said young Alexander. "That's just what I've been seeing, blue gown and all, from soup to finish of this evening. She told me her father bought that little string of pearls on the Ponte Vecchio in Florence, last year, but they wouldn't let her wear it until now."

"Oh, tell me more," sighed Miss Pointdexter, with parted lips. Then remembering the hour, she dismissed the lad, and shut herself in with his white violets.

From that a fresh crop of sentiment and hope bourgeoned in the old maid's heart. She lay awake wondering if she might not hazard a new attempt to bring herself into relation with the Thornes. A mighty longing to see the sole daughter of their house and home took possession of her and nerved her to the effort. The very next day she penned a neat little note in her fine calligraphy, making no allusion to the past or to the fact that she had been so long a resident of New York, and saying it would give her true pleasure to see Alida and Alida's children in their home. And after the note was dropped into the letter-box at the corner, she went on to her place of business, feeling as if green grass were growing upon Madison Avenue pavements.

This time there was no delay in Mrs. Thorne's acknowledgment of Miss Pointdexter's presence in New York. She came during visiting-hours, which of course were Virginia's working-hours, the following day. One card of hers, with one representing Algernon, was left at Miss Pointdexter's boarding-house. On the lady's card was pencilled: "So sorry to miss you. Do come in to lunch on Thursday, at half-past one."

On Thursday, at half-past one, Miss Pointdexter was giving out rolls of work to her waiting women, and when later she called at Mrs. Thorne's, the lady was naturally absent upon her rounds of Thursday teas. Then Mrs. Thorne wrote a note, a kind but manifestly perfunctory missive, in which she deplored Virginia's engagements and her own, said they would fix an early day for dinner, and enclosed a card to Miss Pointdexter for the "At Home," a week distant, when Miss Marion Champe Thorne was to make her bow to her mother's friends.

Before her room had been new papered and her window new hung, in the days when she slept in a painted wood bedstead, not this smart little affair with brass rods and knobs, Miss Pointdexter would not have ventured to think of herself as a possible element of a fashionable New York tea. Now she took it into serious consideration. The chief question was, of course, what this one of the vast army of Eve's self-supporting daughters should wear. Her three-year-old serge, with the new velveteen yoke, and ruffle around the skirt, was dismissed upon its first halting appearance in the line of vision of her mind's eye. Unless Miss Pointdexter of Arcady could go into the world in some-

The Merry Maid of Arcady

thing at least one-half silk, Miss Pointdexter of Arcady would stay at home.

After hours she visited a large shop in Twenty-third Street, where she had been told frocks were to be had, with a skirt well hung, and the stuff wherewith to fashion a bodice, at a moderate price. Eagerly, tremblingly, moistening her dry tongue as she awaited the answer of the young person from whom she inquired the "moderate" price of one of these inchoate garments, Virginia heard it in dismay. Then, boldly, she went down stairs and inquired the cost by the yard of black moiré antique.

To appreciate her daring, the man whose eye passes over these struggles for vanished gentility must be told that moiré antique is a web of pure silk with a pattern like encroaching waves and glistering side-lights; that it has, or should have, a body and consistency betokening long endurance with continuing suavity; that it "comes high," as the shopman told Miss Virginia, after a glance at her modest figure.

That night she revolved ways and means

of getting hold of a sum of money she might spend outright, without regard to her provision for the future. Some time before, young Alexander had merrily told her of his selling to a book-dealer a scarce old edition of "Father Prout," and putting the result into a new frock-coat. Down in the treasure-chest under the old maid's iron bed reposed two or three calf-bound volumes with fine tooled edges that she had brought with her from the wreck of her father's library at Arcady. That they were valuable she knew, but having, some thirty odd years before, been told by her father that he had rather she would not take them from the shelves, it had not occurred to Virginia to turn over their leaves since. At first she thought of asking young Alexander to dispose of one of these, a French book, profusely illustrated, mellow in tint, and altogether rare and fine; but a feeling that she would not like the boy to receive from her hand what her father had forbidden her deterred poor Miss Pointdexter. She bravely offered it herself, turning aside with a pink flush when the dealer looked it over, although, in truth, it was not so dangerous to morals as many a fashionable novel penned by fairest hands to-day. The book-plate examined, the dealer asked, "This is your own, madam, I presume?"

"My father's," Virginia hastened to say, displaying a card. "As I have never read it, I don't know what it is worth. But you will know."

The dealer did know, and to his credit gave her at least one-half what he also knew he could get for it, before nightfall, from an enthusiastic amateur from whom he had standing orders. Virginia hastened home, having withdrawn for a moment behind a rack of volumes to pin in the bosom of her gown the envelope containing the sum she deemed fabulous.

Here I must recall the one evidence of my heroine's unfitness to be a heroine. If a suggestion *did* tickle her conscience that it would be better to put this money aside for emergencies of age and illness, or that she had no right to squander it in dress when others were suffering for want of clothing, Virginia for once in her life turned a deaf ear to the good angel. She resolved to sow one wild oat and be done with it! She bought moiré antique enough for a full gown, and committed it to the hands of a little French woman. Now, a bonnet. "What's a bonnet?" said Miss Pointdexter, dashingly. "Two feathers and a rose." The little French woman had a compatriot—a lesser French woman —who would throw these together for a song. Gloves, five and three-quarters, pale pearl with black stitching, and the old jacket would cover all, and be left in the cloak-room at the house.

While the great affair was pending, Virginia went about her work with a lightness of step, a brightness of face, a joyousness of speech, that surprised those accustomed to her quiet ways. Young Alexander, entering into her affair with zeal, shared her anxiety lest the "second fitting" should reveal some weakness on the untried artist's part, and rejoiced that their common concern proved to be unfounded. "It was the same with my coat," he said, in one of their whispered conferences upon the fourth-floor landing. "The main thing is that your fellow don't pinch you under the arms, you know, and that the tails should be long, but not too long."

"Then you, who go out so much into the world," ventured Miss Pointdexter, while young Alexander expanded under the flattering imputation, "you should know if there is any essential matter to recommend to her. For, truly, she is so determined and talks so fast, I am afraid I have overlooked something I ought to exact."

"There's only one thing I'd tell her to be sure not to miss — a pocket," said the brilliant young Alexander. "Of course, Miss Pointdexter, you are going to let me be your escort to the tea! I want to show you the house a bit, and ask you if you ever saw anything so odd and pretty as a little gold patch in Miss Thorne's hair just where it crinkles on the left side of the parting. You've noticed, of course, that she is the only girl that wears her hair parted, and not chopped off in front: that little white line is as fine and polished as an egg-shell."

Miss Pointdexter here turned the conversation. She could not bring herself to admit that she had actually never seen the fairy about whom the young man daily prattled, and around whom her loving thoughts continually turned like tendrils of convolvulus.

When she found that young Alexander could not leave the office where he was employed downtown in time to do more than "look in" at the Algernon Thorne "tea," Miss Virginia agreed with him to meet her there and bring her home. It was hardly to be expected that *she* could be satisfied with a bird's dip of the beak into this brimming fountain of society, her first social recognition in ten long arid years.

When Miss Pointdexter reached her boarding-house on the eventful afternoon an hour earlier than usual, by especial dispensation of authority, she ran up stairs as lightly as a thistle-down before a summer wind. There on the bed lay the new gown, crisply folded, the new bandbox containing the new bonnet beside it! Blood surged to Miss Pointdexter's head and tingled in her ears — the poor old blue blood, so derided in contemporaneous satire, that had yet done its share to keep the forlorn little gentlewoman's head erect and her heart stanch, in the face of adverse fortune.

It did not seem credible that she, hitherto achieving a new bonnet when the frock was a year behind it, and a new jacket a year later still, should have at once struck the balance of securing a brand-new exterior shell. She shook out the glossy *swishing* folds of the skirt, admired the bodice, took out the trifle miscalled a head-covering, and gloated over them inwardly as a picture-lover does with his Corot or Cazin, a porcelain-collector his hawthorn jar, a book-expert his Elzevir of a first edition. She handled them grudgingly, with sentient finger-tips. She found herself sighing that it was almost a pity to put on her poor frail body objects of art so inspiring, so suggestive. But the toilet achieved, what a transformation it accomplished in the wearer! Even Virginia's modest eyes saw that her little mirror gave back a fashionable dame, one who, she thought, would have been worthy to lie back in the corner of a victoria, or drop in for a cup of tea with no matter who the high-priestess at the tea table. Somebody a day or two since — at this writing it is midwinter — found in the Central Park two dandelions in bloom under a skim of ice. Every year the daring Alp-climber picks fresh edelweiss beneath the snow wreaths, and these fingers have abstracted a lovely bunch of pink glacier-blumen from under an arch of frozen crystal near the summit of Mount Saint Bernard. Miss Pointdexter's sudden expansion of youth and beauty was like these. Her eyes shone, her color came, her whole face and form were instinct with joyous animation. The little looking-glass framed again " The Merry Maid of Arcady."

The Merry Maid of Arcady

Looking out of her window, she saw falling a few flakes of snow — a depressing spectacle in view of the fact that she must proceed on foot to the festal scene. There was no help for it; she must tie up her bonnet in an old brown veil, kilt up her stately trail to walking length, put on her ugly water-proof, and, her glory thus obscured, flit under a shabby umbrella to her old friend's door. Virginia could have hired a carriage but for the treat she had given herself of sending a bunch of lilies-of-the-valley to the débutante.

As she plodded along the slippery, oily street, snow turning to mud as it touched earth, the wind blowing her umbrella rudely, a corner of her new gown escaping to trail on the ground and be gathered up again with difficulty, another woman would have pronounced the game not worth the candle. At the corner nearest Mrs. Thorne's she stood, whipped by the wind, waiting a chance to cross, while carriage and brougham followed each other in slow succession to the awning. Inside these vehicles the faces brought so close to hers wore not at all the hilarious expression to be expected from the possessors of luxurious high-swung vehicles that lift out of the mire and bear so swiftly away from Black Care their fortunate occupants. Haggard, self-sufficient, dull, vulgar, purse-proud; haggard again, again, again; all restless; now a young and unlined face, but even that set with the look of striving after what was not, and with supreme indifference to what was, including little Miss Virginia, who, with the rest of humanity in the streets, stood patiently awaiting the pleasure of fur-caped menials to pass.

At the opera, walking in the streets, driving in the Park, wherever Fashion has her dress-parade, the real man or woman does not show. To behold him or her relaxed into the unpostured self, one must adopt Miss Virginia's attitude toward the favored class.

"Dear, dear," said the little lady to herself, "these can't be the gay folk old Mrs. Parker reads aloud to us about, after breakfast on Sunday mornings at the boarding-house, from that column in the paper that shines in all our eyes!"

When she reached the awning, and pushed her timid way between the broad backs of the footmen lining either side of its opening, the first symptom of stage-fright she had ever known assailed her. It seemed — it *was* so formidable to go up those steps under the tunnel of striped canvas, over the red carpet, already sodden with wet from irreverent feet that had not come in carriages. Nobody noticed her: nobody in New York has time to notice an unfamiliar face: and in this humble fashion Virginia glided across Alida's threshold.

Waved into a cloak-room upon the left of the entranceway, she found the maids all busy, and in a corner, under a Meissonier, she took off her overshoes. A large and supercilious French woman received the bundle composed of Miss Pointdexter's lendings, looking with surprise at the butterfly emerged from a grub. As Virginia followed up the staircase a number of other women, who exchanged little bobbing nods of recognition, and chatted about things seen and things to see, a sense of great desolation took hold of her. In the sea of heads beyond there was not a familiar face. "You will find Mrs. Thorne at the hend of the 'all, madam," mechanically repeated a servant at the top of the stairs. They were in a wide hall, panelled and gilded, and hung with tapestries and living garlands. Virginia, who had somehow thought she might find her lilies-of-the-valley, fruit of true self-sacrifice, in a recognizable place, on a mantelpiece or piano, or the like, and be thanked for them with a smile from her dream-child, felt her little provincial silliness wither at a touch. Such flowers! such numbers, variety, perfume, color — bouquets stacked on every available place — sheafs of lilies, ropes of roses, violets wasting their breath by hundreds; what could be done with them, the brief hour of display over? Oh, the hospitals! the wan or fevered creatures to whose pale hands the touch of one of these ignored roses would bring delight; the dull work-rooms, where young girls comely as any here would conjure poetry and romance on the breath of these hidden violets; the tenement-houses, in whose squalid dusk these unnoticed lilies would shine as fair as the annunciation lilies shone to Mary. And then, drawing a long inhalation of delight, Miss Pointdexter thought of the women like herself, contrasted their joy over the least of this efflorescence with the hurrying indifference of the guests who now jostled by without giving it a glance. Then, confused, charmed, dazzled, a turn of the crowd pushed her before Alida and Alida's girl.

Mrs. Thorne had achieved prosperity and fat. The slim *espiègle* school-girl was merged into the broad-waisted, full-bosomed matron; the skin had reddened; the flaxen locks were dull and few. Beside her, Virginia looked like a slightly ruffled but still perfect white rose. *How* she looked Virginia never thought; the tide of years rushed back, and she was only Virginia clasping her dear Alida's hand.

Mrs. Thorne did not welcome the little show of emotion Miss Pointdexter could not restrain. What a place for moist eyes, for a trembling voice, above all, for a kiss! In the twinkling of an eye she had drawn back, surveyed her old friend with wonder where she got that well-fitting modish gown, noticed that Virginia's hair had not turned, that her teeth were still good, that she had few if any lines around her mouth.

"*So* good of you to come," she said, as she said to a hundred and one others there that day. "You must let me present to you my daughter. Champe, Miss Pointdexter is a lady we knew in Maryland once. You have heard us speak of Maryland."

The Merry Maid of Arcady

At last Virginia looked into the eyes of her dream-child, and felt her hand. None but her own starved self could tell how she longed to find in the girl what she had lost in the mother. She had a glimpse only of the vision young Alexander had described with, for a young admirer, singular accuracy — this rare young girl, standing in her pink robes against a screen of white azaleas; and immediately new names were called, and the very doleful Maid of Arcady was pushed away. She stood in ambush for a while, behind an orange-tree set in a tub, and looked at the heads of the company rising out of a surging sea of velvet and cloth and silk and fur. No one spoke to her. In the Arcady neighborhood, a friend's guest was a friend; here one must have something more than a new moiré antique gown and a place on Mrs. Thorne's invitation list to be recognized. Once or twice, long-

The Merry Maid of Arcady

ing to speak, Miss Pointdexter looked with her ready beaming smile into the face of some woman, crushed and imprisoned in her neighborhood, to be met by an absolutely blank stare. And yet the talk, the clack, went on deafeningly. She had never heard so many plans, so much to do, so much fatigue expressed, so many engagements made for future meetings. Yet nobody spoke to her. And it was plain that among these were the charitable stars, the church members, the famous philanthropists of society — for was not all "society" at Mrs. Thorne's?

"It's a perfect menagerie," she heard some one say. "All sets, all sorts; smart people, politicians, artists, literary folk. They've swept up everybody they know, with a broom, and won't have to be bothered with 'em again this year."

"Why does any one ever come to teas?" answered the lady addressed. "You know how Dr. Holmes describes them, 'Giggle, gabble, gobble, git.' Early in the season, perhaps, when we've forgotten how awful they are since the year before, we may be excused. But after the first half-dozen of the new season, they become hideous — simply hideous!"

Virginia's feet ached before the human current carried her into the dining-room, where several young girls were officiating over tea and cakes and ices. There in a corner she found an empty chair, and dropped into it. A number of young fellows had come in, and were devoting themselves to the tea-makers, and little heed was taken of those who did not push for their own refection. Never in her life had Miss Pointdexter's hungry soul so longed for a kind word, a smile, a recognizing look; the cup of tea that might have acceptably accompanied it was a secondary consideration. What would it cost one of these pretty, dainty daughters of wealth and fashion to step out of her little narrow place in so-called society and drop a crumb of compassion to the unfriended stranger? Why had not their mothers, who had brought them up with every other accomplishment, taken time to teach them that a gracious courtesy of manner may gild refined gold and paint the lily? In her lonely corner, as these thoughts trooped through her mind, Virginia leaned her face into a mound of bride roses and left two pearly tears upon them.

"Here you are at last!" said a cheerful voice, and young Alexander stood before her. She thought he showed well among the other youngsters, so tall and straight, with his moist golden hair forming into a slight wave on his forehead, his kind eyes, his strong mouth curved into a pleasant smile, a flower in his coat. "I asked Miss Thorne if she saw you, but she wasn't sure. But then, with such a crowd coming up, how could the poor girl know one from another? Tea here, please," he added, beckoning a waiter. "I hope you haven't had it."

Miss Pointdexter thought tea would be nectar drunk in such company. She smiled; her face grew radiant. While they were waiting, a gentleman brought an old lady ("One of the war-horses of the smart set," young Alexander whispered slyly in Virginia's ear. "Looks like somebody's cook, doesn't she?") into the room. At once Virginia saw that her old lover was before her. He distinguished her at a glance, and came over, holding out his hand.

"My wife told me you were in town," he said, courteously. "So good of you to come. And I really think you haven't changed a bit. Don't you think the Hungarians are playing too loud? Shouldn't they be further up the stairs? Ah, Mr. Alexander! glad to see your father's son here. The South is very kind to us to-day. We must see you often, Miss Pointdexter; hope you will be here all winter. Yes, those Hungarians *are* too loud. I must go and have them moved. Good-bye. *So* good of you to come."

"Here's your tea," said young Alexander. "Will you take cream or lemon?"

Virginia did not see the servant at her elbow holding a tray; she was in a sort of wounded maze. She turned quickly, and at the same moment the man moved forward. There was a collision, and tea, sugar, cream, sliced lemon, cakes, ices, and bread-and-butter were swept into Miss Pointdexter's lap, and ran in rivulets or formed in islands all over her new gown.

There was nothing to be done but to

get out of the room. Young Alexander, offering ardent sympathy, went with her to the cloak-room, and begged to take her home.

"No; I insist, I *insist*. You sha'n't go back with me when you have only just arrived."

She managed to shake him off, and, hurrying into her old despised water-proof and galoshes and taking her old umbrella, to go away, quite unconscious of the pitying superiority of the maid.

As the front door closed behind her it cut short a wailing strain from the Hungarian band that might well have been the echo of the cry within her heart. The snow fell thicker as the Merry Maid of Arcady pushed her way between the footmen around the awning, and passed out into the night.

Worrosquoyacke

Worrosquoyacke

Part I

ONE evening in November, when the world and his wife and the ramifications of his family, to say nothing of his less-quoted attendants, the flesh and the devil, had surged into the Madison Square Garden for the Horse Show, New York's great social function, Miss Camilla Godfrey sat in a corner of her aunt's box, looking out upon the brilliant scene with a certain weariness of spirit. She was a girl of twenty-one, who had begun her life in society three years before with many aspirations, chief among them the desire to avoid commonplace, and was about to disappoint herself and please her friends by marrying a most conventional man.

Sydney Blackburn, who was consider-

<small>*Worros-*
quoyacke</small> ably past thirty, had exhausted first impressions of many foreign countries, and was now laboriously engaged in trying to find out the merits of his own. He was a well-born, well-mannered, well-to-do club man, not subject to violent emotion of any sort, agreeable in a lazy way, and sufficiently good-looking. Add to this that he had a collection of jades, was an amateur in fine horses, and had recently purchased a stock-farm in Virginia — and one has all that the world in general was able to make out of Miss Godfrey's reputed *fiancé*.

Camilla's aunt, the Countess Cagliari, who sat in a front seat, leaning over the rail and talking in the liveliest fashion to one man after another who stopped to do her homage, although now almost a stranger to her native city, had been a famous New York belle of a generation past. Originally the beautiful Elizabeth Godfrey, younger sister of Camilla's father, and of an influential family of old Knickerbocker stock, she had, about eighteen years before, enjoyed almost a monopoly of quotation as the most original girl in society. People of Camilla's date, who heard this story handed on, tried to imagine any one of their contemporaneous acquaintance holding the palm for anything in New York, and gave it up. There were quite too many white swans in the current now to single out one from among the flock. But people of Elizabeth Godfrey's day had shorter visiting-lists, and knew each other better, and remembered each other's antecedents. They could have told you that, while the Godfreys were still in enjoyment of an autocratic sway over society, Elizabeth, the beauty, was supposed to have been engaged to some man who "threw her over," and had thereupon married Count Cagliari, an authenticated nobleman holding an excellent position at the Italian Court. Left a widow two years before, the Countess had remained in seclusion on the Cagliari estates until her tears were definitely dried, and had now returned to her old home to look with curious eyes upon its transformation. When I say old home, I do not refer specifically to the well-known Godfrey house, the scene of so much entertaining in bygone years, at the corner of ———

Worrosquoyacke

Worrosquoyacke Street and Fifth Avenue. That had been sold upon the death of Camilla's grandpapa, and with fresh paint, large bow-windows, an "American basement" entrance of the approved new style, and an extension with a conservatory built out behind, had passed into a higher state of existence. Of the sons and daughters of the family, all were married and scattered, and the Countess had quite too much knowledge of the world to want, in any case, to take up her permanent abode with one of her brothers or sisters after this interval of separated tastes and habits. So she had hired a pretty flat, stocked it with carved wood and *marqueterie* and gilding and brocade transferred from her Roman palazzo, and had told her brother Charles and his wife to count on her as a chaperon for Camilla, whenever she might be needed.

Camilla, upon first glance at her long-expatriated aunt, wondered how she could ever have been called such a radiant beauty. The rose-bloom of the lady's cheeks had faded, the childlike gold of her locks had given place to a pale ash-brown, obviously thinner about the temples.

There were, even, at times when the *Worros-*
Countess' face was in repose, or when she *quoyacke*
was over-tired, a variety of tiny imprints of
time visible upon its fair surface. But
then, on the other hand, her features were
rarely in repose. Camilla found in her
aunt a most charming animation of mind
and manner. She contrasted her with her
own mother, for example, to the disadvan-
tage of the admirable dame. How dull
Mrs. Godfrey seemed, standing inside her
fine portal at a reception, or presiding over
her large formal dinners, of which three
were regularly given every month of the
season, by comparison with her graceful
sister-in-law, at the Countess' "five
o'clocks" and little feasts that were so
magically pleasant.

Mrs. Charles Godfrey had seen no cause
to regret the sale of the Godfrey patrimo-
nial mansion. She had herself inherited
from her father — a most worthy merchant who had died content without setting foot across the threshold of New
York "smart" society — a corner house
farther up Fifth Avenue, newer and in
every way more desirable, she thought, in

*Worros-
quoyacke* which her husband had quietly hung up his hat upon marrying the heiress. Here, Camilla had always lived, removing to Newport for the summers they did not spend abroad.

Until her aunt had returned to New York, Miss Godfrey had accustomed herself to think of family life as an extinguisher upon everything that offered a gleam of variety in thought, habit, or expression. Her brothers and sisters were excellent reproductions of their mother. Her father, a man of no vivacity of mind, had settled at home into the channel made for him by his wife, and, abroad, found his chief interest in the bank of which he was the reputable head. Camilla, an anomaly in her household, had by now, despairing of changing matters there, begun to think she might better order them to her own liking in her own establishment.

Two of her sisters had already married and were the proprietors of unexciting husbands enshrined behind respectable brownstone fronts. True, the more lately married of them had adorned her brownstone front with a modern stoop, built with steps turning sidewise, and a door half covered with iron grill-work of the most recent pattern; but even that did not enliven Camilla's visits to the house.

Worros-quoyacke

There had not been lacking suitors for our difficult young lady's hand. There had been two proposals in New York and one in Newport during the past season (as her mother was fond of narrating to her spouse), either of which would have been as good a match as Laura's or Charlotte's. But Camilla thought if she could do no better than Laura or Charlotte she would coif St. Catherine's tresses for all eternity. Her brothers-in-law — who were in reality estimable young men — excited in her the liveliest sense of boredom. Laura's boy failed to interest her, and Charlotte's girl, who was the image of her papa, sent her young aunt out of the nursery with a new perception of the vacuity of earthly joys. And now, in spite of all, she was said to be engaged to Sydney Blackburn.

Before my poor heroine is condemned as a very unreasonable and morbid young person, let me make haste to explain that, in her eyes, the crowning offence of the

Worros-quoyacke good people who composed her family circle was their worship of, and blind submission to, the petty standards that control a very small circle of metropolitans — a sadly common complaint, indicating a mental state that would be summed up by a plain-speaking person like Thackeray in the plain word "snobbism." Mr. Blackburn was, at least, no snob.

What a comfort it had been to find in her gracious and charming Aunt Elizabeth a quick understanding of the things that vexed Camilla's soul. Far too well-mannered to make plain comment upon the weakness of her form-loving American relatives, Madame Cagliari yet allowed her niece to feel her tactful sympathy, and to be sustained by her superior judgment in all such matters. To-night, as they sat together looking down upon the crowded promenade encircling the ellipse, and around at the rows of boxes where fashion rioted in grotesque form and color of attire, Camilla met in the older lady's eyes an expression of dismay answering to hers.

"My dear girl!" she exclaimed, "the

half had not been told me of the exuberance of overdressing here. Why, most of them have come in velvet and lace and satin to what is actually a stable-yard! How dull we must appear in our plain little tailor-gowns! Pray look at the outrageous woman coming toward us in the crowd. The little fat one, I mean, who has those enormous frills to her cape and bows on her hat of every color; why, I beg your pardon, it's your sister Charlotte."

Worrosquoyacke

"Yes, it is Charlotte," said Camilla, woefully. "And she is perfectly satisfied with that outfit because she had it of Madame Léonie, who dresses the De Veres. Laura's new costume is just as bad, and they are both charmed with them. What can I do, Aunt Elizabeth?"

"Nothing, if they are happy. Believe me, my dear, it is only in America that people carry the sins of their near relations. It is *rococo* to be sensitive upon such minor points. There goes your father, my good brother Charles. Even if he has that crumpled, office-worn look so many New York men wear in middle life,

<small>*Worros-
quoyacke*</small> he is handsome and *distingué*, and you, my child, get your looks from him."

"I never wanted to look like a Godfrey so much as since I have known you, Aunt Elizabeth," said the girl, smiling.

"Here comes our friend, Blackburn, after his survey of his hunter who is to jump presently and win laurels for his master. Do you know, Camilla, I like my future nephew immensely."

"Wait until he is your nephew before you feel obliged to approve of him," answered her niece, coloring a little hotly.

"What are you going to do with him, if not marry him? After all, he is a gentleman, he has no affectations, he does not stake his earthly happiness upon what other New Yorkers do and say; he will make an admirable husband, and you can travel half your time."

"I recognize those facts," said Camilla, briefly. Further than this no one had yet brought her to go in discussing the probabilities of her future relations with Sydney Blackburn.

As he came up the stairway nearest them and along the passage behind the

boxes, the two women saw that he was *Worros-*
accompanied by a young man of surpris- *quoyacke*
ing and unusual good looks. Of medium
height, slim of figure, erect with a suggestion of military training, the stranger's
clear pale skin and rather melancholy dark
eyes, his dress more unstudied than lacking in tidiness, the cut of his waving
brown hair — all suggested a place of
origin far remote from his present surroundings; but that he was a gentleman
in the true old-fashioned sense of that
much-distorted word, nobody could for a
moment doubt.

"Where did Blackburn get his hidalgo
from?" whispered the Countess, hur-
riedly. "Or, no; on the whole he looks
to me as if the part of him we see in the
crowd ought to belong to a well-bred
Centaur."

Blackburn's prosperous middle-aged figure, his slightly bald head and pale yellow
mustache, made a sufficiently marked off-
set to the appearance of the stranger, whom
he at once presented as Mr. Richard Wilcox of Virginia.

"Mr. Wilcox is my nearest neighbor

Worros-quoyacke on the plantation I have acquired so recently that I need him to tell me all sorts of things beside my proper boundary-lines," Blackburn added pleasantly.

"I have myself long been absent from there," the young man said. "And when I came back a year ago, from a wandering life in New Mexico and Arizona, to try farming a deserted inheritance, you can imagine how glad I was to find Mr. Blackburn the purchaser of the next estate."

"I like that; you still call them estates down yonder," said the Countess, gleefully, but without malice.

"I suppose it sounds absurd to you," answered Wilcox, a faint tinge of red perceptible in his cheek. He had fallen quite easily into the chair behind Madame Cagliari, leaving Blackburn to take that nearest Miss Godfrey. "But we can hardly call them farms, when it takes several farms to make up one of them; and 'place' is a vague sort of term."

"Call them by their proper names, of course; estates they have always been since they were crown grants to those lively ancestors of you Virginians, who were hurried out of England for their country's good, perchance."

Worrosquoyacke

The airy lightness of her tone robbed the words of the sting they might otherwise have had. Wilcox smiled.

"That's the comfortable Northern version of our antecedents, I am aware," he said. "But they were not all of that stripe. I have been led to believe mine were a very decent kind of immigrants."

"And they left you a princely establishment down there on the banks of the —what is it?—James, thank you, in which you fared sumptuously and were a model for all other Americans, and brought up hundreds of slaves to bless the day when they were born captive in your service, that is, 'befo' the waugh.' Am I not well-informed?"

"With some slight modifications, entirely so. Our home was never princely, but it was delightfully big and jolly. I, unfortunately, was born 'after the waugh,' and therefore know the old days only by tradition. My father was an officer in the Army of Northern Virginia, who fought

Worros-quoyacke through most of its battles to return home and find himself a ruined man. He was engaged to my mother at the time, and married her on the understanding that if they could not get a living out of the old acres, without the slaves, they would emigrate, which contingency in due time occurred."

"Why do you stop?"

Wilcox hesitated. He did not care to admit that, his eyes at that minute falling upon Miss Godfrey, he had detected upon that fair creature's face a look of the most undisguised curiosity in his affairs. "Am I making myself ridiculous in thus babbling?" he asked himself rapidly.

"Pray go on," said Madame Cagliari, in a tone that was a command.

"Oh, nothing — that is really all there is to tell. I was born on a Texan ranch, and, strapped to a saddle-bow, I began my roving. I have done little else. I got my education from my mother till she died, then from my father, then from an old Padre at a mission near where we lived longest in New Mexico. I have never been through a university, and I know nothing, absolutely nothing, of the great world. I suppose Blackburn thought it would be an experience for his friends to see an aboriginal in contrast with all this," and he made a motion toward the brilliant ring of boxes.

Blackburn, who was talking to Camilla, indifferent to the fact that she remained with her gaze fixed upon the newcomer, caught his own name.

"Eh! You are telling the Countess you are going to ride Lady Sweetlips for me presently. But then she will show for nothing beside your Di Vernon, Wilcox. With you on her, by George, that beauty of yours will leave everything behind her in the high jump."

In his enthusiasm Blackburn drew near the Countess, and for fifteen minutes held the conversation in a technical discourse upon the respective merits of his mare and his friend's. During this interlude, the Countess listening with her ever-ready, well-pleased smile, the young Virginian moved over to sit in the seat behind Miss Godfrey, to occupy which, indeed, he felt himself bidden by some imperious,

Worrosquoyacke

Worros- swift telepathy he was at a loss to under-
quoyacke stand.

"You wanted me to come here?" he said, blunderingly. "I beg your pardon, I should not have said that. I meant, I suppose, it is the custom for a man to change seats with another when he has claimed a lady's attention long enough."

"Tell me about your mare," she said, blushing slightly, much against her will. "She must be a rare treasure if Mr. Blackburn accords her such praise."

"She is a darling — my best friend!" the young man exclaimed, with an enthusiasm Camilla had never before seen in one of his sex and age. "I bred her down there on the plains and taught her everything she knows and named her out of an odd volume of Sir Walter Scott that made part of my shelf of books. I would never have yielded to the vanity of bringing her to show off here, but that Blackburn overcame my scruples, in fact, persuaded me into it. But now, Miss Godfrey, do you not think I have talked quite enough of myself and my own; I do, and I can't understand why I have done so."

At that moment there came into the box *Worros-*
a lady attended by two dapper youths. *quoyacke*
At the spectacle of this homely old woman
in a girlish costume of dark green velvet
and chinchilla—to whom her young followers paid court as to a maiden in her
first season — Richard Wilcox allowed his
ingenuous face to express the wonder of
his soul.

"This won't do, d'ye see?" said
Blackburn, presently linking his arm in
that of the young man to draw him from
the spot. "Who ever before saw a fellow show so plainly what he thinks of old
Mother Thomson? Your eyes are telltales, my dear boy, and I must take you
away from the chances of betrayal."

"How can women like Miss Godfrey
and her aunt associate with that — person?" asked Wilcox.

"Why, my dear Rusticus, that is not a
person, but a personage. There are more
like her to whom the aspirants for place
bow down. In the eyes of her followers,
she shines with a lustre which has nothing to
do with the native woman. She is a leader,
a social law-giver; and that's enough."

Worros-quoyacke

"She — she is not a friend of Miss Godfrey's?" inquired Wilcox in a rather scared whisper.

"No, certainly not. Camilla Godfrey is an independent, an eccentric, if you will. She has no patience with such as that. But Countess Cagliari is more used to strange apparitions in good society. She takes Mrs. Thomson as a necessary condiment in the salad of New York. If you had looked at Miss Godfrey at the moment, you'd have seen her pretty face grow cold and hard."

"Did it, by Jove, how glorious!" exclaimed the younger man, so loud that people in his vicinity turned to see to what he was alluding.

"Gently, Wilcox, we are not on the plantation, remember. I see I was right in my intuition that you and Miss Godfrey would meet upon common ground. She is, without your excuse for it, in the same defiant attitude towards things — well, not all things — established that you are."

"You mean, then, that she despises sham and pretence and petty affectation. Thank God, I have met one such in this fountain-head of American form and fashion where they seem to me to be utterly un-American in fundamental principle. Blackburn, it is all true that you told me about that girl over our pipes by the old dining-room fireplace at home. She is wonderfully lovely, fresh, and witching; yet I think she looks dissatisfied. She is evidently wrestling with some problem still unsolved — coming to some determination about which she isn't at all sure of herself."

Worrosquoyacke

"Gad, he hit me hard there," said Sydney Blackburn to his inner man.

"The other one is of the real sort, too, although she ran me a little about old Virginia when we first began to talk. One feels she could never do a mean or a low thing, and her manner is fine — such a dainty smile, and so sure of herself."

"From whom did he get this power of discrimination about women?" Blackburn was wondering for the twentieth time since their acquaintance began. "A fellow who was literally born and brought up in the wilds."

Blackburn had first encountered Richard

Worros-quoyacke Wilcox in the preceding spring, when upon a first visit to his new possessions on the bank of the James River. The young man — living alone in the half-deserted mansion handed down to him from his forefathers, his household an ex-slave woman and her husband, the latter the army-servant of the late Colonel Wilcox, C.S.A. — had been a Heaven-send in the way of companionship to the sociable New Yorker. Their common interest in horses, and Wilcox's superior information on points in which Blackburn had to own himself still an aspiring amateur, confirmed the intimacy then begun. They had corresponded, Wilcox had been of substantial service to Blackburn once or twice in looking after the movements of his man in charge of the Virginia farm, and, finally, after many solicitations, had consented to come to New York in the autumn as Sydney's visitor.

Dick's meeting with Mr. Blackburn's friends brought about, as it appeared, quite casually by him, was, in reality, a test of some moment to Sydney, that easy-going philosopher. He wanted particularly to know how a girl of the peculiar bent of *Worros-* Camilla Godfrey would strike the very *quoyacke* straightforward young Virginian, who had a way of applying his Ithuriel's spear to pretty much everybody with whom he came in contact. For Blackburn, who had so long resisted the wiles of agreeable femininity in so many lands, was not now in a hurry to let himself go without full and due satisfaction as to the wisdom of such a course. He was in love, after his fashion, with this girl who treated his advance so coolly; but he had no desire at his age to make a fool of himself, and the effect she had had upon Wilcox now cheered and stimulated his passion exceedingly. He determined, at the earliest convenient opportunity, to allow Wilcox to know the truth about his pretension to her hand. Perhaps walking home that night after the Horse Show, perhaps while they were smoking in his sanctum, whose Oriental magnificence may have excited wonder (not revealed) in the breast of the visitor, and to whose cushioned divans and filigree Moorish arches Master Dick had adapted himself with infinite ease. Wilcox should certainly be told. Wilcox deserved to know among the first. Wilcox would be a pleasant acquaintance for Camilla when she should go down to Virginia to stop at the old Manor House Blackburn was then having fitted up by experts from the North. She would enjoy riding with him through those cathedral aisles of the pine woods, and boating and fishing under Dick's superintendence on the river. He had seen in Camilla's eyes that she approved — as she rarely did any man presented her — Mr. Blackburn's new-found friend.

Blackburn was right. Camilla did approve of Wilcox, with a strange leaping of the heart she was confounded at having to experience. When he left the box, Mrs. Thomson, looking after him, had drawled, "And who is your Orson, my dear child? Really, now, if Blackburn could persuade him to have his hair cut like other people, I almost think I would say he might be brought to my Monday evenings."

At this Camilla, in her ardent, imprudent way, fired up and said things that caused Mrs. Thomson to write her down on the side of her book devoted to people who are to be severely let alone. This was the more rash of Camilla, as most of the inner circle of the smart set had rather be snubbed and insulted by Mrs. Thomson than actually left to their fate without her. If Camilla's mother and sisters had heard the passage-at-arms between the older and younger lady, they would have trembled and turned faint at the prospect of Camilla's future. But that nice, comforting Aunt Elizabeth preserved her pleasant, inscrutable demeanor, and when Mrs. Thomson and her body-guard beat a retreat only said, with laughing eyes:

"Do you think, shocking child, that handsome boy, we shall probably never run upon again, was worth your banishment to Mrs. Thomson's Siberia?"

"It was not for him, but the principle, dear," Camilla began, and stopped abruptly. Madame Cagliari did not pursue the subject. A number of other visitors claimed their attention. The evening wore away, till Camilla, who had been consulting her programme, settled back in her chair and fixed her gaze eagerly upon the ring.

Worros-quoyacke

The high jumping for gentlemen riders was about to begin, and Madame Cagliari, following with her glass the direction of Miss Godfrey's eyes, saw a light, elegant figure seated upon Mr. Blackburn's well-known Lady Sweetlips, cantering back and forth beneath them.

That Sweetlips, the darling of her master's heart, won her due meed of honors, would be naturally a gratifying thing to Miss Godfrey. But Camilla's aunt was unprepared for the charming radiance of satisfaction that overspread the young lady's face and manner. She thought she had never seen Camilla look so pretty and girlishly happy before.

"Blackburn will be coming to receive your congratulations," said the Countess, but the remark fell upon deaf ears. There still was Camilla intent upon the ring, leaning forward in rapt delight. A mare and rider had now made their appearance, upon whose first trial round applause from the audience arose irrepressibly. The mare was a grand, free-stepping creature, black as jet, sensitive to a touch, and humanly intelligent, as any one could see, who, when presently put to the test of the *Worros-* bar, went easily higher and higher, until *quoyacke.* her flight through space seemed merely a question of when her rider should bid her attempt the feat. There had been nothing like it seen that night, or any night, in the Garden. The audience as one voice broke into cheering until the judges would have no more of it, and the next event was placarded. Before leaving the ring the rider and mare passed around under where Countess Cagliari sat with her niece, waving him a greeting with their handkerchiefs. A salute so slight that they alone recognized it, expressed his thanks, and he was gone.

"Did I not say truly he is of Centaur build?" exclaimed the Countess, now more excited than her niece. "My dear Camilla, if our young man knew what is to his advantage, he would never get down from that saddle to become a mere commonplace mortal again."

"I am delighted that you had this opportunity of seeing a specimen of Wilcox's horsemanship," Blackburn said, by-and-by, when he again joined the ladies. "He is

Worros-quoyacke of that old-time breed of Southern riders who are as one with their horses, and is able to execute quite an astonishing variety of feats when in the saddle and at full run. But those are not his only attractions, as you will find out if I succeed in persuading you to come down to visit me on the plantation. The old house he lives in, and his relations to things generally, will interest you I am sure. He is just now undergoing a bombardment of civilities to himself and that mare of his, and could make a small fortune out of the sale of her if he were so disposed."

"But he will not part with her?" asked Camilla.

"Hardly," said Blackburn, with a grimace. "I have found that out, on my own account, long before this. Come, Madame Cagliari, while the Virginian scheme is again upon the tapis promise me that you will make up a party to be my guests, at any date you may fix before Christmas. I want your verdict—a woman's verdict —upon some of the improvements I'm making in the house, but there is enough finished to give you comfortable quarters.

I think Mr. and Mrs. Godfrey will not *Worros-*
object to entrusting their daughter to your *quoyacke*
care for the jaunt, and there are a few
other people I believe we can get, who
will make up a congenial house-party for
a week."

"It is most enticing, certainly," said
the Countess, covertly consulting the expression of her niece. To her surprise
Camilla was in a condition of beaming
acquiescence.

"Yes, yes, we will go. I know papa
and mamma will make no objection," she
said eagerly. "I have always wanted to
have a glimpse of that romantic old life of
Virginia still under the cloud of war when
all our part of the country has so long
passed out of it. Besides, what you have
told me of the neighborhood, the climate,
and the outdoor life is like a whiff of fresh
air in a hot room. Do say yes, Aunt
Elizabeth, and let Mr. Blackburn fix a
time when he will be ready to receive us."

"We shall see," answered Aunt Elizabeth, in an approving tone. Blackburn
was quite taken by surprise by the readiness of Camilla's acceptance of his scheme.

Worros- Surely, this could mean but one thing, and
quoyacke his staid, elderly heart began to be invaded
by a new and encouragingly active sensation of delight.

As they sat in the smoke-room of Blackburn's sumptuous flat an hour later, he was impelled to bestow his confidence upon young Wilcox. But, somehow, this was not altogether an easy task. At Sydney's age, a man beats about the bush for words in which to clothe an announcement involving sentimental relations with a young and blooming maiden.

At last in despair, he did what he had better have done in the beginning — blurted out the fact that Madame Cagliari and her niece had promised to visit him in Virginia; and then, before he had had more than time to note the apparently exhilarating effect of this statement upon his friend, followed it up by these unvarnished words:

"And you know, Wilcox, or you ought to know, if you've half the insight I give you credit for, that I'm expecting Miss Godfrey to go there one day as my wife."

Wilcox did not move a muscle, but smoked his cigar in silence to the end.

"Wilcox did not move a muscle, but smoked his cigar in silence to the end." p. 80.

Then with a brief "I congratulate you," *Worros-* he bade his host good-night and left the *quoyacke* room.

"Odd fellow, that," said Blackburn. "Never does the things one expects of him."

Part II

Worros-quoyacke

"THERE is no host like a well-bred bachelor," said Madame Cagliari, when, after the luncheon the day following their arrival at Pampatike, the ladies assembled in the library to have their coffee and await the coming of the men. "I can't think why, when some women bestow their very best efforts upon entertaining, they miss making their guests as deliciously comfortable and as much at home as we are now."

The architect-decorator, sent on from New York to carry out the scheme of restoration in the old dwelling, had certainly acquitted himself with credit of the task. Never a "stately home" of old Virginia, Pampatike House was now as it had been in its palmiest days — a livable, cheery place, with its wooden wainscotings and corner cupboards and spindle banisters and egg-and-dart mouldings, renewed under a lustrous coat of cream enamel paint; its deep brick fireplaces freshly reddened; the dark floors polished and waxed, and strewn with Turkey rugs of the old lost shade of soft crimson; the furniture-covers and curtains of red moreen in the same tint, the tall old mahogany bookcases refilled with books in antique bindings.

Worrosquoyacke

"An ideal lodge in the wilderness," went on the Countess in her soft, approving voice. "And in my room there are crewel-worked bed-curtains, a knot-work quilt, and a pair of bedside steps, such as I have always coveted. They must have ransacked all the old curiosity shops in Washington and Richmond to fit up this house."

"What stories the old furniture and ornaments could tell of bygones in the different families they came out of," said Miss Godfrey, with animation. "If we could understand their true feeling it would probably be one of protest against us as usurpers, and against themselves as pretenders arrayed here together out of place."

Worros-quoyacke

"Bah! This house belonged to nobody in particular," said a mocking lady of the party. "It was originally built for a bailiff, I believe, attached to estates of the Wilcoxes, who were the grandees in these parts, and was added to by some member of that family who wanted to live in it. Mr. Cleve, who has been here before with Blackburn, tells me the 'real thing' to see is that old gone-to-seed mansion of the Wilcoxes with the extraordinary name I can't remember —"

"Worrosquoyacke?" queried Camilla Godfrey, sitting up erect in her three-cornered armchair with the brass claw-feet.

"Yes, that is it — Wurrusqueak the negroes and country people call it. Well, Mr. Cleve tells me it is something no one ought to miss who wishes to see one of the best specimens of early Colonial architecture still extant. But the trouble is to get inside the house. There is only a young man living there now, poor and proud, and a couple of former slaves of the family to take care of the house and master. The young Wilcox would not relish a horde of us descending upon him, I fancy. Not unless he could entertain us, that is; and he is about as well able to do that as the gentleman with the falcon, who killed and cooked his pet bird to serve his lady's table."

Worrosquoyacke

"How immensely interesting!" drawled a woman whom Camilla Godfrey hated on the spot. "I should like so tremendously to go there, and see him just as he is — a last leaf trembling on the bough of ancient aristocracy. Now, dear Miss Godfrey, you have more influence than any of us with Mr. Blackburn, do persuade him to make up a party — a raiding party we will call it — to descend unexpectedly upon the gentleman with the squeak in the name of his place. Really, if you don't, I shall try coaxing Mr. Blackburn on my own account."

"I shall leave it to your eloquence," said Camilla, freezingly. "Nothing would induce me to obtrude myself under such circumstances."

"No doubt Mr. Wilcox, whom I have had the pleasure of meeting," said Madame Cagliari, "will himself give us an invita-

Worros-quoyacke tion. If there are old pictures — a Kneller, I'm told — still upon panelled walls, and a room full of rare china, the owner would certainly consider it a favor to us to exhibit them."

"Now, why can't I say things like Aunt Elizabeth," meditated Camilla that night as, in reviewing this conversation, she sat before her dressing-table, "instead of flying off the handle as I did, and always do? Of course, she took the right view of it. He must come — he must ask us to go there. I shall see his home, his surroundings that have haunted my imagination ever since I met him first. I can't think why I should have presumed to be disappointed because I saw or heard nothing of him when we landed on his shores. And why have I been waiting and watching all day in the hope of hearing Mr. Blackburn say when and where we are to meet him? Not a word, not a sign, from him. Oh, suppose — suppose he should not be at home!"

With this, Miss Godfrey relinquished the three parts of a massive plait of bronzed hair she was weaving for the night, allowing it to break up in a ruddy glory over her shoulders to her knees. As she caught sight of her eyes in the mirror they seemed to her to be smitten with alarm too deep for words. Then with a sudden revulsion she laughed, but not exactly a merry, light-hearted laugh, and, recapturing her locks, began anew her soft toil of plaiting them.

Worros-quoyacke

Miss Godfrey's vigil over night did not, however, affect her readiness next morning to ride after breakfast with her host. Blackburn, who had promised to show her a stretch of old Virginia woodlands so enriched with moss and crowsfoot, with laurel and pine, and huge hollies in full array of living green and crimson fruitage, as to banish the thought of winter's reign, felt satisfied that his experiment in bringing this young lady to behold her future kingdom was a success. He had never seen her so alert, so joyous, so full of interest in her surroundings as now when they rode swiftly through the scented green arcades of the pines, talking of the vicinity, its people, its traditions.

Worros-quoyacke Everything that Sydney could tell she listened to with eager comment. And by-and-by, when a horseman came out of a cross-road and rode up behind them suddenly, Camilla felt herself start, then blush with an eagerness of expectation she feared her host might notice.

"Hallo, Parson!" exclaimed Blackburn, pulling up for greetings and introduction of the rector of Worrosquoyacke Parish.

An ex-soldier, and every inch of him proclaimed the fact that soldier he had been — was the Reverend Emilius Fauntleroy, despite the clerical cut of his rusty black suit, the trousers half-concealed by leggins of green baize, called in Colonial times "splatterdashers." Having fought through the war to emerge with a few honorable scars, the Doctor did not now concern himself greatly with affairs outside of State politics, his poor, his quaint old Colonial church, and the steed or two he always managed to keep in his stable — his stud now consisting of an ancient "buggy" horse and the fiery young colt he was at present breaking to the saddle.

Like everybody else in the neighborhood, Doctor Fauntleroy had heard the rumor that among the guests of the Pampatike House party was the lady of Blackburn's love; and relishing a love affair, like all other good Virginians, he now rode at Miss Godfrey's saddle-bow, his eyes twinkling with satisfaction in the *rencontre*. Blackburn, who had begun to find Camilla's thirst for information, historic and genealogical, beyond his powers to satisfy, challenged the rector to supply his deficiency; and it was not long before she was put in possession of the leading facts, present and past, of the annals of a quiet neighborhood. The rector, with whom all such things were a hobby, did not perceive the special interest expressed in his hearer's face when he touched upon the subject of the ancestral home of the Wilcoxes, its chimneys now visible not far away, on a wooded bluff near the river.

"That's a house worth showing you," the good gentleman went on, twisting in his saddle to point out a momentary glimpse of brick walls, half hidden by evergreens

Worros-quoyacke upon a sweeping lawn. "What do you say, Blackburn, to our taking the young lady inside for a peep at the woodwork of the main stairs and the pictures in the dining-room?"

"I had been rather expecting Wilcox to ask us all to see them," said Blackburn. "I sent an invitation over there yesterday to him to dine to-night at Pampatike, at the same time I asked you. But, unlike you, he has not given us the pleasant promise of his company."

"He's from home, you know. Went to Richmond yesterday morning. Too bad the boy should not be here to profit by a little good company of his own age and standing. I did hope, Blackburn, you had succeeded in pulling him out of his reserve. But, by George, sir, lately he's worse than ever. However, his absence makes no difference, as far as seeing the house is concerned. You know I was Dick's guardian, and am, besides, his kinsman. I can answer for it he will be proud to have Miss Godfrey honor his bachelor quarters, and old Sylvie will thank God when the gentry set foot over her threshold. Did you chance, Miss Worros-Godfrey, to meet my lad when he was in New York?"

"Yes," faltered Camilla, turning her head to look down a forest vista. On no account must she show the tumult of her feeling.

"I really think you will enjoy the house better under Doctor Fauntleroy's guidance than with any one else," said Blackburn in a matter-of-fact way. "I know your dislike to doing anything in parties, and if we do get another chance to go there you will be at an advantage over all of them. I'll swear I am vexed, though, that Wilcox should have given us the slip. When he comes back and finds you have been to Worrosquoyacke he will be well punished."

"Do you really think we should go?" ventured the girl, hardly knowing how to frame her protest.

"Why not?" asked the rector. And "Why not?" echoed her host — queries she could not answer. In her blank and bitter disappointment nothing just then seemed of much consequence. She let

Worros-
quoyacke

them open gate after gate for her passing, and at last rode under an archway of ancient iron-work bearing the Wilcox coat-of-arms, into an avenue of noble denuded trees that led up to the front door, feeling herself the creature of an elusive yet rather fascinating dream.

This, then, was his dearly loved home; this large, rambling old pile built of mottled brick, the roof swept by the black, leafless branches of great trees; the long array of windows closed and shuttered; the stately front door, up to which they passed over a flight of worn marble steps, hermetically sealed. In response to the rector's vigorous and resounding attack upon the knocker no sound of life within was heard, and the vexed gentleman was about himself to go around to the rear when a wheezing cough inside proclaimed old Hannibal, the major-domo, one of Dick's solitary pair of servants.

"I'll bet you any money," said Doctor Fauntleroy, quite innocent of his unclerical offer, "that goose, Sylvie, saw us coming and kept Hannibal to put him into his old claw-hammer coat that was made in the time of Henry Clay. You will like *Worros-* Sylvie, Miss Godfrey. She is one of the *quoyacke* truest souls and most transparent old idiots now living."

The door swung open and Hannibal appeared, so attired as to realize the rector's prediction, bowing to the ground in welcome. A little in the rear stood Sylvie, vast and turbaned, her black face aglow with reverent rapture. Having acquitted herself of the honors of reception she waddled away, leaving gray old Hannibal to usher the guests within.

Not even the morning sunshine blazing through a wide east window could make the inside of Worrosquoyacke House cheerful to look upon. During the war this ample hall had served over night as a stable for the invaders' cavalry, and the defacement of walls and wainscoting had never been repaired. The lovely sweep of the double staircase, with its balusters like Chinese puzzles in ivory, soared away out of the cracked marble of the floor into a circular hall above, under a rotunda of patched glass, which, during the war, was so broken that birds had nested inside on

Worros-quoyacke the tops of doors and windows. When they passed into a large drawing-room veiled in gauze and holland, containing furniture, ornaments, and mirrors of value and great beauty, Camilla shivered at the desolation of the place. It was not until they recrossed the hall and entered a large dining-room filled with family portraits and solid pieces of mahogany furniture, gray for want of polish, that signs of human habitation relieved the sense of gloom. A desk, an armchair, a sideboard whereon a few bits of beautiful old Queen Anne silver caught Camilla's eye; books scattered everywhere, and a pair of fire-dogs mounting guard over a bed of hickory ashes upon which Hannibal speedily kindled a new and noble offering of logs, all testified to the habitual presence of some one not a ghost. While the rector detailed for the visitors the history and traditions of the Wilcox family gallery, Camilla's spirit turned aside to speculate upon these daily haunts of the absent young master of the house. So intensely did her vivid imagination play around the object of her thoughts that it was hardly a surprise when a door

in the wainscoting opened and Wilcox, in
person, with a pair of cocker spaniels at
his heels came into the room.

For the young man, who had been pursued in his morning ramble by an envoy of Sylvie and brought back to receive his guests, there had been some preparation for this meeting. But in Camilla, surprise, vexation, and other emotions met and almost robbed her of speech. Hardly were the explanations of their belief in his absence from home met by his assurance that he had set out for Richmond the day before — but, changing his mind, had returned late the previous night, and was just sending off an answer to Blackburn's note — when Miss Godfrey, looking out of the window at the horses in charge of Blackburn's groom, announced that she really could not keep those creatures waiting another minute to set off.

"You must first let Sylvie offer you some of her pet cherry cordial," said Wilcox, with a rather melancholy smile. "The old woman charged me to make you wait for that, and for a shortcake now preparing. And, to while away the

Worrosquoyacke

Worros-quoyacke time, let me show you the china boudoir in the visitors' wing, where the rooms are dry and in excellent preservation."

"Do you take the young lady to see the china, while I show Blackburn these books we found last week in the garret," said the rector on his knees before the lower shelf of a bookcase.

Camilla, her habit caught in one hand, stood the image of beautiful uncertainty; then, yielding, accompanied Dick through the drawing-room into a long, glazed and matted gallery hung with sporting prints and St. Mémin profiles, thence into a wing containing half a dozen rooms, of which the windows outside were almost overgrown with ivy, as well as shaded by the trunks of tall magnolias with their foliage of glossy evergreen. .

"Does it make you nervous, this ghostly green light?" said he, noting her little shiver. "I suppose I ought to have the ivy cut away and sacrifice a tree or two, but in summer these rooms are so deliciously cool. Besides, there will be no one to occupy them in my time — and after me, the deluge!" he finished, pulling up suddenly.

They were standing close to each other *Worros-* upon the hearth of a faded boudoir crowded *quoyacke* with the accumulated treasures of several of Dick's china-loving grandmothers. All about the two young people the atmosphere was surcharged with pathetic suggestions of decayed fortune and forgotten life. As Camilla, keenly feeling these things, fixed her soft gaze upon the young man who seemed to embody what so strangely attracted and moved her in his home, she did not know that she, in turn, appeared to him as a breathing embodiment of all that his life lacked. The glowing pulse of youth, hope, sympathy, beauty — it was like a draught of fresh water to thirsty lips. He stopped short in the conventional explanation he had begun to make to her of the contents of the room, stammered, and was again silent.

"Pray tell me more; I am most interested," she said hastily.

The consciousness of unspoken sentiment between them affected her also; so much so, that, womanlike, her impulse was to take refuge from it in rapid speech. But the young man, ignoring her words,

Worros-quoyacke continued to look at her with unspeakable content.

"I think we must go," she went on, startled at the revelation in the sound of her own voice, and moving toward the door.

"No, no! Don't go — when I rode all the way back yesterday, against my better judgment, on the mere chance of getting a glimpse of you. I'm not coming to Pampatike. I can't. If you stand where you are just five minutes more I will never ask you to do anything else for me. After this there will be nothing to try for. But I'd be a poor sort of creature if I could not endure."

As if under a spell Camilla remained, her eyes drooped before his, till the hush of the little low-toned, lavender-scented room became intolerable. She was hoping he would say only a word more, anything that would free her tongue. But no word was spoken, and at last, with a quick repellent gesture, she darted away from him, and before him, into the entry and along the matted gallery.

Part III

ONE morning at breakfast time, about a year after these occurrences, Dick Wilcox came into his own dining-room to find there the rector, who, having tied his nag to a rack outside, had stepped in unannounced.

Worrosquoyacke

"Ha, Dick! Caught you napping, didn't I?" said the Reverend Emilius in his hearty voice. "I came early because I want to talk to you."

"Always glad to see you, Parson," said Dick, shaking hands with his visitor. "But you'll wait a minute till I order in the provender?"

From the dining-room to the belonging places of cook and butler there had once been the necessary bells, but these were broken long since, and when Dick desired to inform his servants that he was ready for a meal, he accomplished it by opening a door and shouting, "Oh! Syl-

Worros-quoyacke vie," at the top of his hearty young lungs. This act now accomplished, simultaneously Nip and Tuck, the spaniels, sent up a vociferous barking, awaking the echoes of the silent house.

Upon the remnant of a fine old damask table-cloth Sylvie, arriving, deposited a dish of broiled bacon, delicately curled, with a crisp corn-pone, brown of hue, a pat of butter she had just churned in a bottle, and a tin pot of coffee emitting delicious aroma. Whatever was lacking at Worrosquoyacke it was not good cooking, so long as fat Sylvie's pin-cushions of brown hands were there to manipulate her scant material.

"I've had a surprising letter from Blackburn," said Doctor Fauntleroy, when the old woman had disappeared to prepare one of her famous omelets.

Dick's hand was steady as he set down his coffee-cup.

"Then he is back in New York again?"

"Yes, and says he will be here for Christmas with Mrs. Blackburn. The letter was principally concerned with the affairs of that rascally agent of his, whom we have just seen the last of, and the personal news was confined to this mere announcement. I suppose the marriage took place in Italy, where Miss Godfrey has recently been visiting and travelling with her aunt, which accounts for our not having had the details, *ad nauseam*, copied from the New York papers into our local sheets. That is one of the benefits of our isolation, in my eyes. Well, I suppose, Dick, we shall have to furbish ourselves up to do honor to the bride, charming creature, but too young for Blackburn, according to my thinking. I have already told my good old Belinda to send my Sunday suit to the cleaner's in Richmond, and I've an idea, my boy, that it's about time for me to invest in another pair of shoes. What! is that the best breakfast you can manage?"

"See here, Parson, I've made up my mind this farming the old acres will not do for me," answered Dick, getting up to walk to and fro beneath the concentrated gaze of his unremunerative ancestors ranged around the walls. "I was meaning to talk to you about it. There's an old chum of mine in Texas writing me to come down

Worros-quoyacke and go into a land speculation with him, and I think I'll accept."

"Small blame to you, my lad, to want to leave this dull neighborhood," said the rector, kindly. "But bide awhile longer, Dick, I've hopes of a better chance for you than that. Blackburn, who is a capital fellow, has been busy working up a scheme for you in New York that, if I hadn't pledged myself not to unfold it, you'd soon see is well worth your while considering."

"I cannot consider it," exclaimed the young man, hotly. "I decline to be Blackburn's beneficiary. I shall go South at once, and, if I see there is nothing in Scott's affair, I can return here later. No, Parson, don't try to coax me. You, if any man, should understand that when I make up my mind to a thing it is settled. But I don't mind telling you there are reasons why I cannot take such a favor from Blackburn and retain my self-respect."

"Reasons?" persisted the rector. "Why a year ago you and he were as thick as thieves, and if your friendship has fallen off since it can only be because Blackburn has been away globe-trotting."

"If you must know, he has just married the only woman I ever loved or ever can love," said the young man, stopping short beside the rector's chair and looking him full in the face.

Worrosquoyacke

"Good gracious!" said the Doctor. "Am I blind or ossified that I did not find this out before? Since when, Richard, has it been going on?"

"Since I first laid eyes on her," answered the young man, simply.

"Then I muffed it, didn't I, when I brought her over here last year?" went on the bewildered rector.

"You gave me, on the contrary, the quietus I sorely needed. Since then it has been plain sailing. But I'm not ready to take material advantage from her husband. Oh, no, Parson, that's not like a Wilcox."

"If you want to know my opinion," quoth the rector, after the interruption of Sylvie's arrival with her omelet, "it isn't like a Wilcox to run away in the face of a crisis. No, Dick. Stay here and see her and let yourself be cured for good, as you will not be if you go off and dream of

Worros-
quoyacke

her. Blackburn writes that his wife wants to see a Virginia Christmas, and that they will bring friends as before. We must do our part, for the credit of our State. The least you can do, dear boy, is to invite them here to break bread with you for once."

The rector had his way, and after dark on Christmas Eve saw the "great house" at Worrosquoyacke in an unwonted stir of preparation for company. A powdering of snow capped the hollies and cedars of the lawn; the air was crisp and invigorating, and stars shone in a brilliantly clear sky. Along the final stretch of the avenue leading to the house Chinese lanterns were tied to the low branches of the trees, and at intervals between them were stationed little colored boys, each ineffably content with the consciousness of a box of matches in his pocket, and the sense that at a given signal he was to be part of a show. In the old hallway the scars of war and time were covered with screens of wildwood greenery, with boughs of crimson-berried shrubs, with garlands of laurel and crowsfoot. For Hannibal and Sylvie well understood the old-time methods of decoration for a "party of gentlefolks," and to aid them in preparation had convened half the black folks in the neighborhood. Improvised frames for candles upon every doorway were garnished with leaves of magnolia laid one upon another, like the wreaths upon great Cæsar's brow. The large drawing-room, rid of its shrouding bags, was polished and warmed and lighted brilliantly. All day long Sylvie had been proudly conducting to its threshold, to view its glories, deputations of her own color, whose rapturous admiration filled her soul with content. On the upper landing of the stairs were seats for the musicians, a band of negroes, who were presently to bring into their performance the soft cries and hand-clappings, the time marked with their feet, that makes their dance-music often well-nigh irresistible.

When Dick had informed her that he was to offer on Christmas Eve a supper to the new Mrs. Sydney Blackburn, who would that day arrive in the neighborhood with a house party of friends, the old woman had gained two inches in stature. And when, putting into her hand a sum

Worros-quoyacke

Worros-
quoyacke

of money that Dick knew, and Sylvie knew, and each knew the other knew to be extravagantly in excess of what he could afford, he bade her spread a table that should be a credit to her housekeeping, Sylvie accepted the trust with silent resolve to do or die. What if he went without afterward, thought the poor lad, so long as his lady was honored fitly? And it should go hard with her if she and the old man couldn't scrimp to make up for Marse Dick's outburst for the honor of the house, thought Sylvie.

Thus for to-night had come back to Worrosquoyacke the old baronial cheer of long vanished days. The mahogany dining-table, re-enforced by other claw-footed supporters, revealed to the combined gaze of ancestral Wilcoxes their once familiar dishes and beakers and flagons of antique silver, set upon it after the manner of supper-tables of the gentry in Richmond, as Sylvie remembered them before the war. At one end a huge block of ice set upon a platter was hollowed out to receive raw oysters. One of Hannibal's best hams, rubbed in hickory ashes some three years before and brought to the perfection of the nutty flavor he deemed desirable, now stuck with cloves and garnished with a cut-paper ruff, occupied the other extremity of the board. Between were jellied chicken and tongues and a substantial round of "huntsman's beef," cured after Mrs. Randolph's famous receipt; game, hot and cold; croquettes and salads were presently to be added with a "hen's nest" of eggs made of blanc-mange in a bed of quivering jelly, the hay simulated by cut lemon peel; charlotte russe, and other tremulous and deliquescent sweets. There was even a rumor that ran with ecstasy down the line of lantern lighters outside of ice-cream in store, enough for the black folks after the "quality" should be fed.

Worrosquoyacke

Dick, called in by Sylvie just before the arrival of his guests to survey his feast, found her with Hannibal radiant with pride. Not for worlds would Sylvie have let any of her retainers without see her do it; but, once inside and the door shut, she lifted high her hands and voice:

"I bless Thee, Lawd, that Thou has

<small>*Worros-quoyacke*</small> let Thy sarvants see this sight in ole Wurrusqueak House agin befo' they dies."

And Hannibal, closing his eyes, devoutly said "Amen!"

"There ain't but one drawback to it, Marse Dick, darlin'," went on the old creature, fondly. "This here's the spit en image of a weddin' supper, an' here's the best-looking groom on Jeamses River, ef I do say it as shouldn't. Ef there only was a bride fitten to mate with him."

"Hush, old woman, don't talk nonsense," said the young man, his cheek reddening as he walked into the hall.

At this moment a light twinkled far down the avenue, another, another, then two lines of them, then a bonfire of pitch-pine shot up a glare of radiance upon the façade of the old brick house. Dark faces and forms that had gathered from all quarters to see the fun were revealed in unsuspected numbers. As the first carriage drove up before the wide open front door, Dick advanced bareheaded to greet his guests.

There were two occupants only of this vehicle — Blackburn and the Countess Cagliari. In the little excitement of greeting

them, and going to meet another carriage
from which stepped two women robed in
long furry wraps, and two men he did not
know, who immediately joined the first
arrivals on the portico to await the rest,
Dick could do no more than stammer a
few words in Countess Cagliari's ear:

"Your — your niece is not coming
then?"

"Of course. Camilla is in the next
carriage. You have no idea how eager
we all were to accept your hospitality and
how much Mr. Blackburn and I were
charmed with this compliment. The old
house is like a palace in a pantomime to-
night, with all these lights — music, too?
How I love that negro music. It is like
nothing else. What a welcome to dear
old Virginia! No, I assure you, you could
have done nothing to please us half so
much — my husband has always — "

"My wife is thanking you for both of
us, eh, Wilcox?" interrupted Blackburn,
coming up genially and putting a hand upon
the shoulder of the late Countess Cagliari.

What he said more, what anybody said
or did, just after that, poor Dick could not

Worros-quoyacke have testified to on oath. He stood stock still, the blood surging to his temples, his heart beating violently, till a carriage door opening gave into his very hand the gloved fingers of Camilla Godfrey, who sprang to the steps and turned toward his a face made up of beaming joy and maidenly reserve. There was no speech between them, for, after the Pampatike party, came neighbors thick and fast — neighbors in all sorts of vehicles from the old pumpkin-colored chariot with unfolding steps, let down from inside the doors, to a mule wagon filled with young fellows and pretty girls seated upon split-bottomed chairs and making the night air resound with their gayety. Dick had his hands too full with greetings and congratulations upon the reopening of his house to pay especial heed to any one. Before the wide hall fireplace, wherein burnt a giant Yule log covered with lichen and bearded moss, the new Mrs. Blackburn stood between her husband and her host. Dick was struck with the happy, restful look upon the lady's mobile face, while her grace in receiving their friends was never more apparent.

At the first convenient interval, Parson Fauntleroy, with a quizzical gleam in his eye, whispered in Dick's ear:

"By George, sir, we were nicely taken in. When I told Blackburn just now that to the last minute I'd believed he had married the niece, he laughed as heartily as if such an idea had never touched his brain. He even had the cheek to tell me it was a year ago down here at Pampatike that he fell in love with the widow. And he says, Dick, he wrote me all about his engagement from Cairo last winter and told me to tell you. Of course, we must believe Blackburn; but I'll bet any money — I mean I'm pretty sure — he forgot to post that letter if he ever wrote it. Never saw a fellow more in love, though. Why, Dick, it makes me think there's somebody somewhere in this world waiting for an old bachelor like me."

The Reverend Emilius slyly took this turn to cover the glowing excitement his words had produced in Dick. But as just then the music struck up and the leader of the band called out persuasively, "Gentlemen will please seleck their ladies and

Worros- take their places for the fust set," it was
quoyacke the host's duty to lead off the guests of honor into the drawing-room, to open the merry ball.

The good rector moved away chuckling to himself. He had not thought it necessary to tell Dick that Blackburn had also communicated to him the business offer he was prepared on the morrow to make to young Wilcox in due form — an offer of prospective independence to be won in fashion so congenial that Parson Fauntleroy had no words in which to couch his satisfaction with Dick's good luck. As the dance progressed, the rector, standing on the outskirts and looking well pleased, happened to catch sight of the portraits of Dick's father and mother, both appearing from amid their Christmas garlands, likewise intent upon the scene, and a lump came into his throat.

"Their lives and fortunes, poor things, were part of our great sacrifice," he said within himself. "Thank God, their boy has ' outsoared the shadow of their night.' "

At last Dick was free to seek her. They danced together, and at the end of it he

The Holiday Dance at Worrosquoyacke. p 1:3.

asked Camilla to go with him to the well-remembered china-room, into which Sylvie, with artistic sense of color, had put only pink shaded lamps that, with a little fire of oak branches upon the dragon andirons, gave to it a new feeling of warmth and cheer.

Worroswell-quoyacke

Standing there again upon the faded Turkey rug before the fireplace, they went back together step by step over the months that had separated them. At his solicitation, Camilla, in delicious fashion, told her tale of wandering abroad with her aunt until they were joined at Cairo by Mr. Blackburn, after which the Countess' engagement to that gentleman was made known to every one concerned, and the marriage arranged to take place in Rome in the following November.

"Ah! Why did I not know?" interrupted he, fiercely. "Why have I lost all this time?"

"Could I write to you?" she asked archly. On her, now, there was no sorrow of the past that weighed. "Besides, when Mr. Blackburn told Aunt Elizabeth that he had informed Doctor Fauntleroy,

<small>*Worros-quoyacke*</small> and no answer came, pray what was one to think?"

"But you knew — oh, tell me you knew," he went on with eager passion in his tones, "that I loved you and wanted you from the first — the very, very first. Would you have given yourself to me, here, a year ago, — just where we stand, — Camilla?"

"You expect me to admit everything," began the girl, trying, as girls will, to keep at bay the moment of surrender they know is at hand.

Directly after this a Dresden clock upon the mantel-shelf chimed twelve. Outside arose a babel of sounds: horns, torpedoes, shouts. The negroes around their bonfires were bidding welcome to Christmas morn. Simultaneously, upon the threshold of the boudoir, appeared a little round-eyed darky, an offshoot of Sylvie, sent by his grandmammy to summon his master to lead in the march to supper. But, as this small person heard the sudden noise without, habit overcame borrowed ceremonial, and with a joyous cadence in his voice he cried:

"Chrismus' gif', Marse Dick!"

And Dick, who, from the beautiful, happy eyes and lips close to his had just received his own Christmas gift, did not say the saucy rascal nay.

Worrosquoyacke

Leaves from the Diary of Ruth Marchmont, Spinster

Leaves from the Diary of Ruth Marchmont, Spinster

Part I

BY 9 A.M. this morning, I had finished my breakfast, and was off to the meeting of our branch of the Charity Organization Society, where I gave in my report of visits among the poor, heard the other reports read, and then walked briskly down Fifth Avenue to Washington Square, and home to Thirty-fourth Street, in order to get my muscles into play and my lungs full of fresh air. It was gloriously crisp and clear; the best sort of spring weather in New York. As usual, I made note of all that was passing in the street, and amused myself wondering why so many clever people of my acquaintance find ours such an uninteresting city. To me, every paving-stone and chimney-pot

Leaves from the Diary of Ruth Marchmont, Spinster

is of interest. But then I was born here, and my people before me were citizens and a part of the local system of things, and our importance has grown with the growth of New York. My grandfather, in early life a thrifty and reputable merchant, amassed wealth, became mayor of the city, won the respect of the whole community, and, as I remember the old gentleman, was a kindly, simple-minded, public-spirited man. Until after his death, however, the family had not had the habit of spending money. My father, indeed, was brought up in trade, and had no college education. He married the pretty daughter of a thriving druggist; mama was ambitious; their children had every advantage of training; and to-day we are among the social leaders of New York. But, somehow or other, I am an outsider in the show. When mama gives her great crowded receptions to which all the fashionables come, instead of enjoying myself like the rest of them, I wander through the crush, and note this one and the other one, and speculate about their personality, their aims, their antece-

Leaves from the Diary of Ruth Marchmont, Spinster

dents, and the unfitness of so many of them for the high place they occupy. Something seems lacking — perhaps it is in me; and yet I do not think I am a morbid or unhappy girl. Mama and my sisters say I am a faddist; a hypercritic, who is not satisfied unless she is finding fault with established things.

Let me see what I can jot down of a single day's experience, and then try to judge of the whole.

After my walk, I went for an hour to draw at the Art League, and brought home from there to luncheon with me a girl in whom I am exceedingly interested, — Mary Challoner, of Southern birth and good family, charming to look at with her clear darkness of complexion, her eyes so darkly blue, and her profuse silky black hair, the finest little feet and hands ever heard of out of a fairy book, — and of the most marked good breeding in manner and appearance. The Challoners, I have ascertained, are dreadfully poor, — have drifted to New York to try to make a subsistence. This girl has great talent with her pencil, — so much so, that the rest of us at the

Leaves from the Diary of Ruth Marchmont, Spinster

League fall back and gaze on her in despair; and she has also a surprising gift of song and improvisation. I have fallen into the habit of calling her Corinne, and the others have taken it up. For some time, I've been coaxing her to come to our house, but only to-day would she consent. When we got here, I took her at once to my own "bachelor" quarters, with the sitting-room opening out of the tiny bedroom, both littered and crowded with things I have picked up in curiosity-shops and travel. After her delight was a little sated, we went down to luncheon. On the threshold of the dining-room, with its antique tapestries and carved black Venetian furniture, she paused, and drew a breath of satisfaction. "Why, it is like an Italian palace." "It all came out of an old Italian palace, bodily," I said, laughing. "Oh! how I love great dusky spaces and mellow backgrounds," she went on, and the little thrill in her voice made the girls, who were already sitting at the table, turn and look at her in surprise.

These were my two sisters, Martha and Elizabeth, and the Hamilton-Hooker twins,

Leaves from the Diary of Ruth Marchmont, Spinster

two members of the "smart set" much esteemed by our family. Mama was away at a great lunch party somewhere; and, as I introduced Miss Challoner to the others, I said something in passing about her talent. One of the Hamilton-Hookers actually put up her glass to look at my friend,—both barely nodded,—and they and my sisters at once resumed their conversation about the "bicycle tea" at Claremont. From that moment, my sweet Corinne was as much ignored among them as if she had been a disembodied spirit. I saw she felt it, that her color came, that she could not eat; and, although I redoubled my efforts to be friendly with her, the wound was none the less deep. Directly after lunch, she went away, and they did not vouchsafe an allusion to her. To them, a person out of their set was simply of no earthly interest, and they had not tact enough to feign what they did not feel. I, who have grown tired of reasoning with my own family on such points as these, shut my lips and said nothing. But I ask myself "are my sisters and the Miss Hamilton-Hookers fit to be models in good

Leaves from the Diary of Ruth Marchmont, Spinster

manners to the country at large? If there were a reform in society, would they be among those who are to dominate the new regime?" For we need reform, and quickly. Who is to bring it about, I know not, but I believe the day will come.

Later that afternoon, a young man called and was kept waiting in the hall. He was a shabby young man, with bright eyes and a handsome eager face. One of the footmen who had admitted him, gauging him by his coat and hat, had very contemptuously awarded him a seat upon a three-cornered affair of marble ormolu that my father calls the "chair of torture." There he sat, forgotten, till I, passing through the hall again saw him, and asked the reason of his delay. He was the brother of our little nursery-governess, Miss Smith, and, having an hour before leaving for the West, had called to spend it with her. When I heard how he had been ignored, I *charged* into my mother's morning-room, to which she had just returned from the party uptown. She was tired, her face was flushed, she looked stouter than ever in her costly attire of lace and jet. Full

Leaves from the Diary of Ruth Marchmont, Spinster

of complaint against the length of the entertainment of which she had partaken, she would hardly listen to my tale. Her maid, busy in taking off her street costume, warned her there was barely time to change to another dress that lay upon the bed, in readiness for her day " at home." " See Miss Smith? I think that is quite too much," she exclaimed, angrily. " When Miss Smith is the only person who can keep those children in order, and the house is just about to be filled with company. Besides, the children must take their walk. Go at once, Maria, and tell James to excuse Miss Smith to her visitor." Throwing myself into the breach, I pleaded to be allowed to take the children out; and, for once, carried my point. I knew that mama, who is kind-hearted when not in too great a hurry, or pressed by the observances of fashionable life, did not mean to be unjust. The little governess went off joyfully to walk with her brother, and I took in charge the bevy of youngsters who gave me as much as I cared to undertake in the way of mental and physical exercise until five o'clock.

Leaves from the Diary of Ruth Marchmont, Spinster

Then I dressed hastily, and went down stairs. The rooms were well filled,—mama's usual "menagerie," as papa and I sometimes jokingly call it. Mama, standing near the doorway, was kept busy receiving newcomers, which she did, however, in a perfunctory way, saying little to her guests beyond the conventional "How do you do." Poor dear! she can be lively and agreeable enough, when she has time, but her life is one long straining effort to keep up with the rush. My sisters, at the tea-table, looked lovely, and were dressed in the perfection of good taste. I am always proud of the girls in public, they are, to look at, such charming types of modern American civilization. But I can't say I like the men they choose to bring around them, and to invite to the house. It seems to me that, with our position, our education, our ample means, we might have *such* delightful people here; and, from week's end to week's end, no one comes except those few whose names are repeated over and over in the doings of fashionable life. Nor do I admire my sisters' manners to their guests. If they

Leaves from the Diary of Ruth Marchmont, Spinster

are interested in conversation with some of the young men in question, they make no effort to be polite to any one else. Older people, especially, are coldly offered tea, then left to shift for themselves. My sisters, apparently, believe themselves to be of a caste set apart from the ordinary necessities of civility to, or exertion in behalf of, others.

A little woman came in and spoke to mama effusively, to whom my mother returned a rather measured greeting. At once, I identified this newcomer as Mrs. Dorval,—the wife of a clever and rising young professional man,—who has seen a good deal of society during the past winter. When we first knew her at Bar Harbor, some years ago, she was a fresh, lively creature, with a great deal of social tact, witty and original, rather proud of her success in compassing effects with small means. Recently they appear to have had a little increase of income, and she has made a bold dash into fashionable life. They have moved into a new house, give dinners, and she is indefatigable in being seen everywhere. People like

Leaves from the Diary of Ruth Marchmont, Spinster

mama, who have everything they want, give her only scant encouragement, but still she is getting on. Remembering Mrs. Dorval with pleasure, I advanced to greet her. During the little time we stood talking under a portière, I found it impossible to rivet her attention to any subject, so eager was she to nod to, and be noticed by, the passing show. Out of her talk every particle of originality has gone. She asked me the usual questions. Had I been to Mrs. X's dance? Was I going to Mrs. Z's reception? Did I know that it is whispered the Y's are to be divorced? In her eyes, I thought I detected a weary look. I know it is said the Dorvals are living beyond their means. I wonder if what they are getting out of this venture repays them for what has gone into it. Surely, Mrs. Dorval — for I believe her husband is not responsible — is not a fair type to fit into the reformed society for which we ought to hope. In that blest assemblage, like will fraternize with like; the iron pots and the earthen pots will swim down the stream in company with their own kind, not together. I believe half the discontent I see around me now comes from the attempt of mediocre fortune to pattern itself in all things like the great.

Presently, arrived old Mrs. Thompson, the wife of one of grandpapa's former partners in business. She, like ourselves, is very wealthy, and lives in a fine house uptown with richly woven shades of *écru* lace at every one of her front windows, and a front door that is all stained glass and ornamental iron-work. But she is not "in society," and, after mama had shaken hands, she was quite at a loss what to do with her most recent guest. Then espying a young man standing by unoccupied, — a young man who had dined with us over and again, had sat in our opera-box, and spent weeks with us at our house in the country, bringing his valet and his horse, — she beckoned him to her.

"Please take Mrs. Thompson into the other room, and tell Martha and Elizabeth to give her some tea," my mother said. But the gilded youth, muttering something between his teeth, turned on his heel, and left us.

Leaves from the Diary of Ruth Marchmont, Spinster

Leaves from the Diary of Ruth Marchmont, Spinster

"Ruth, remind me never to let that man be asked here again," mama said, in an undertone. But I knew she would relent, and that he would be asked again. With all my heart, I hope his variety will be eliminated from the good society of the future.

Taking the old lady in charge, I started for the tea-room, and there, to my satisfaction, she met Mr. Ledger, one of grandpapa's old clerks, whom my mother declares papa *will* keep on asking to the house, when there is no longer any reason for it. Mr. Ledger was drinking lemonade, and eating ices, and nibbling at various little cakes. He looked very happy, and much honored when I consigned Mrs. Thompson to his care. I do believe that, to Mr. Ledger, mama and Mrs. Thompson are quite in the same grade; but I am glad mama is not aware of the fact, or Mr. Ledger would then never be allowed to nibble any more little cakes at our house.

When I turned to go back to mama, I overheard two people discussing the dining-room. "Such an affectation to try to make it all seem old," said one of them. "Were you ever in their other house? Anything more frankly *bourgeois* was never seen than that establishment. And they only moved ten years ago." "How we apples swim!" said the other voice. "But all her grandeur cannot make the mistress look like anything but a chambermaid. The girls are well enough, though the oldest one *is* a little touched in the upper story, and they suppress her in consequence. But they are all spoiled to death, and need a good taking-down in consequence."

Leaves from the Diary of Ruth Marchmont, Spinster

And these were my mother's guests, at that moment engaged in eating her bread and sharing her salt. In the reformed society, I hope it will be out of date to talk against one's hosts, until, at least, the visitors who so desire to express themselves have reached the sidewalk.

Then I was stopped by Mrs. Delamere, who fancies herself much more to the manner born than we are, and is patronizing in consequence, though, as a fact, they have the start of us by only one generation. She is a large, plain-spoken,

Leaves from the Diary of Ruth Marchmont, Spinster

rude woman who, in some way or other, has recently set up as a "Patriot's Grand Daughter," or something of the kind, and has bought a lot of old china and old mahogany to refurnish her dining-room, with row upon row of brand-new "Copleys" and "Gilbert Stuarts" and the like upon the walls; and these she calls her ancestors.

"Is it true, my dear, that your mother has made application to become a 'Patriot's Grand Daughter'?" she asked me, in a high and cutting voice. "If so, you being the brains of the family, as they say, should warn her that she will have a perfectly horrid time trying to get in."

"You certainly should know," I said, unable to resist it, and wickedly rejoicing to see her wince. As I moved on in the crowd, I felt humiliated that everything conspired to place us in a false position. In actual truth, mama had never dreamed of being a "Patriot's Grand Daughter," though I don't know what she may do, by next year. Just because we are spending our money liberally and intelligently, and patronizing art in decorating our house,

Leaves from the Diary of Ruth Marchmont, Spinster

why must we be taunted with aspiring to be what we are not in American society. Surely, these things will all have to be readjusted before we attain the ideal.

At that minute, one of the footmen presented himself at my elbow. "If you please, miss, do you think I might be let off to go away home? I have had word that my wife is very bad, and there's a new baby, miss, that's come before its time, and I can't get a chance to ask Mrs. Marchmont's leave to go." I at once reported the case in my mother's ear. It was in the interval between the batches of guests, and she looked tired and bored. "Thomas, is it? How very tiresome. Of course he will have to go; but there are people to dinner and we need him later. Tell him to come back if he possibly can, Ruth. Who knows if the whole thing is not made up? I have been so often deceived by that class, I can't trust myself to feel sorry for them."

Thomas escaped with an alacrity and an expression upon his face leaving me no doubt that he was in earnest. But mama was not all to blame for her lack of

Leaves from the Diary of Ruth Marchmont, Spinster

sympathy. Time and again we have been taken in, egregiously, and made to regret our kindness to his sort. While I was reflecting upon the fact that in every department of our present mode of living, the same unreality crops up to confront us, Mrs. Mammon made her appearance in the room, attended by the last new sensation in society in the way of a titled foreigner. This was the Vicomte de Videpoche, so notoriously unfitted for the society of decent people, that I felt a rush of indignant blood come to my face when I saw him take the tips of my mother's fingers and bend over them in salutation. Somehow or other, I thought of Poe's story of the "Masque of the Red Death" coming into the room, and how all the revellers fell away from before it. But here was Mrs. Mammon smiling and chatting with him and introducing him to people on either side of her passage through the rooms, and everybody, without an exception, smiled on him in return. Regaining my mother's side, I again whispered in her ear. "Mama, dear, if you love me, give that dreadful man a snub. Don't let him think you are among the American matrons he has upon his string." "Ruth, you worry me to death!" exclaimed my parent, perhaps justly. "And I don't know what you mean by a dreadful man. Vicomte Videpoche is received everywhere, and he is going to dine here this evening." "Then I stay up stairs," I said. "And oh! mother, I would give anything in the world I own to prevent his daring to speak to one of our girls." "I should think you might trust your father and mother to judge of such things," she said resentfully. "If you are going on this way, I think you had better stay up stairs. Girls in these days are entirely too much inclined to meddle with things they should know nothing about; and, for my part, I call ideas like yours decidedly unfeminine, if not worse."

A little later, some one tells me the newest *on dit*; that Videpoche is engaged to Mrs. Mammon's eldest daughter, and their wedding will be the *most* brilliant affair that has ever been chronicled by the New York newspapers.

After that, while people came and went

Leaves from the Diary of Ruth Marchmont, Spinster

and I said the civil thing to those of them I knew,— for I am literally unknown to half my mother's friends,— I felt disheartened and lifeless. All of the glory, the love of living, I had brought in from my morning walk had vanished. The atmosphere around me seemed to be surcharged with the spirit of shame.

At this point, my hand was taken by my old friend Mrs. Gardiner, before I knew she was near me. "What a beautiful, ideal home you have, my dear," she said, in her sweet, cheery voice. "And how the contrast with it must strike you in some of those poor flats you and I make visits to. By-the-way, I have had an anonymous subscription to our Working Woman's Recreation Fund, that takes all care off my mind for the rest of the summer; and I do believe it came from that good father of yours. Your mother, too, sent us a new piano unsolicited, for the 'Home.' I felt so grateful, I had to come here; though I confess I rarely put in an appearance at a 'tea.' I often wonder, Ruth, if you and I realize how many good people there are to care for the poor and helpless in this community that is so much maligned for its shortcomings. Come with me to the University Settlement to-morrow, and we'll have a cosy talk in the carriage going down." "I am so glad you came," I said, rather incoherently; "I needed something to restore the balance of my spirits, which were down all on one side. Yes, I will go, to-morrow; and, between us, we shall try to find types of the higher civilization of New York, with which to populate a certain Dreamland I have in mind of a society that is to be wholly lovely and of good report." "I am always interested in your dreamlands," she said, and my heart warmed at her smile; "and never fear but we shall find your types."

Leaves from the Diary of Ruth Marchmont, Spinster

I was just feeling a little ashamed of myself, when the apparition of one of the Hamilton-Hooker twins, followed by the other, in the doorway beyond mama, renewed some of my rebellion against the artificiality of life.

"Those girls," I said to Mrs. Gardiner, "are to me among the most trying specimens of our dominant society. Their

Leaves from the Diary of Ruth Marchmont, Spinster

handsome faces are like masks of self-satisfaction and indifference to outside humanity. They are so convinced they are made of superior clay, that many people have ended by conceding as much to them. My sisters look up to them, and copy them, which is the chief reason of my animus in their direction. Really, Mrs. Gardiner, I doubt if either one of them ever knew what it is to perform an unselfish or self-sacrificing action."

As the second Miss Hamilton-Hooker came into sight, following her sister, we saw that she had, leaning upon her arm, a very old gentleman, tottering, asthmatic, blear-eyed. This was a well-known character of New York society, their grandfather, once a famous beau and dandy, now a butterfly upon his last flights, anything but agreeable in his physical peculiarities, and yet possessed with a mania for going where other people congregated. As the crowd pressed this pair near to us, I heard him say, querulously, that he wanted to sit down and rest a bit; and I was astonished at the quiet good temper with which Louisa Hamilton-Hooker guided him to a chair, and placed him in it, standing there and taking pains to point out people, and chat to him about them.

Simultaneously, a man joined them, and I recognized Delancey Jones, who, report says, has been playing fast and loose with Louisa's affections, these two seasons past. He is a handsome fellow, could give her the position she expects in marriage, and on this occasion I saw a blush of satisfaction at his approach appear upon her placid countenance.

"Like to go into the room where the new pictures have been hung?" he said, negligently; but her eyes flashed joyful assent, and at once she started to accompany him.

"Give Louisa her chance, and she'll win," a satirical voice whispered near me. Others than myself were watching the little show.

"Louisa! Louisa! I want you to tell me about all these people," wheezed the shaking grandfather, plucking at her sleeve.

Poor Louisa looked about for her sister, who was not to be seen. Then, with a sort of appealing glance to the superb

Leaves from the Diary of Ruth Marchmont, Spinster

Leaves from the Diary of Ruth Marchmont, Spinster

Delancey to remain with them, of which he took no manner of notice, she declined his invitation and watched him saunter off.

"That's well! Send him away, send him away. Deuced uncivil fellow, anyhow. You stay with me, Louisa; and tell me when anybody comes along I ought to speak to," piped the little old gentleman.

As Louisa bent down quite patiently to obey him, I saw something very like the glimmer of tears in her porcelain blue eyes.

"We sha'n't exclude Louisa from *all* our privileges, shall we?" asked Mrs. Gardiner, smiling in answer to my own thought.

Part II

*Bar Harbor, Mt. Desert Island, Maine,
August, 189–*

JUST a year ago our new house at Newport was finished; and, after getting rid of the workmen with infinite difficulty, and installing in their places all the beautiful furniture and bric-à-brac she had brought from abroad to put into it, mama threw open her stately establishment for a ball, at which "all the world wondered." Columns of eloquence about the decorations, the illuminated grounds, the flowers, the supper, the toilettes, filled the papers of the day. The affair was undoubtedly the "smartest" of "smart" functions. Mama confessed to the family afterward, that she could not help comparing it with the tea-parties her own mother used to give in Brooklyn, when mama was a young girl; where they had soda-biscuit, and frizzled beef, and peach preserves, with ice-cream

Leaves from the Diary of Ruth Marchmont, Spinster

Leaves from the Diary of Ruth Marchmont, Spinster for a crowning treat. Somehow or other, I always like to hear about those tea-parties, and my good, plain grandmama at the head of the table "pouring out." But it is the rarest thing in the world for mama to speak of them, in these days, now she is a great lady of the New York plutocracy, and her children are so ultra-fashionable in their ideas; all except homespun Ruth, who persists in leading an independent life, and in thinking for herself.

The desire of mama's heart had been that great house at Newport. To secure it, she first made papa forsake the "cottage" at Long Branch we once thought so very swell, and rent one at Newport, season after season, until gradually he was brought around to the idea of building there for himself. The result was a stone villa of the most exquisite beauty in design, erected by one of our great architects; and, in one year, the landscape gardeners and florists brought the grounds to external perfection. The bills staggered even my long-suffering and generous father; but they were paid, and the opening ball was given; and last season

Leaves from the Diary of Ruth Marchmont, Spinster

was passed by us in a blaze of fashionable glory. Just what we had been doing all the winter in New York, we did over again at Newport. We drove, we visited, or went to luncheons and musicales and afternoon parties, every day; in the evening there were dinners and balls, at all of which mama made a point of being seen with her younger daughters. My sisters Martha and Elizabeth are beauties, and consider themselves *fin-de-siècle* in all respects. As papa says, they take to all this grandeur as ducks take to the water; though that is an illustration mama regards as vulgar. I, only, Ruth, aged twenty-five, thin, dark, nothing much to look at, a book-worm and a dreamer, fail to do credit to the Marchmont display before the eyes of society.

What I started out to say was that, after their extremely brilliant and successful first season in our new house, my father naturally expected to see his wife and daughters return there to occupy it this summer. But to his surprise, mama announced, early in the spring, that her rheumatism made it absolutely necessary

Leaves from the Diary of Ruth Marchmont, Spinster

for her to try a German bath-cure, and that rather than be separated from the dear girls, and the nursery children, they would all spend the summer abroad. Accordingly, the Newport house remains shut up, for mama is quite too great a lady to think of letting her domicile for another family to live in. Early in June, the "Paris" took over in her best deck staterooms, Mrs. Marchmont, the Misses Marchmont, the young Masters and Misses Marchmont, a variety of governesses, maids, and *valets-de-place*, with a mountain of luggage that will be increased after they pass through Paris coming home. Papa, and my brother John who is at college, and I, went off to a farm we have in New Hampshire, where I am to rejoin them later. And I then accepted the invitation of my friend Mrs. Wentworth, whom no one can help loving, to spend August at her cottage at Bar Harbor.

We arrived here last night, my maid and I, after a tiresome journey from Boston. But all the way I was saying to myself: "What a delight to escape the trammels of Newport conventionality, and

Leaves from the Diary of Ruth Marchmont, Spinster

go to a place where nature is the supreme charm!" Often as I had heard of the rock-bound island in northern seas, where mountains rise directly from the chafing sea, and views are beautiful, and air is life-giving, I had never been here. My fashionable friends had so often said to me: "After Newport, Bar Harbor is such a delicious rest." More than one artist has told me that everything here is so picturesque, and at the same time within the scope of eye and imagination. As we sailed hither yesterday across the bay at sunset, and I saw the rugged range of blue mountains rise against softly radiant sky, I went out alone on the deck, forward, and silently took it all in, in thankfulness that I am at last permitted to enjoy it. Here, I said, we shall be far from the madding crowd of gayety-seekers. We shall live abroad, tramping the hills in loose mountain costume, or boating and canoeing upon this sapphire sea.

At this juncture, a young man whom I had met last season at dinner, Hugh Elliott, who was standing near me on the deck, turned, identified me, and took off his hat.

Leaves from the Diary of Ruth Marchmont, Spinster

He, too, was on his way to spend a month at Bar Harbor, and, as an old frequenter of the place, he undertook to point out the localities, and give me any such information as I desired. I was glad to meet Mr. Elliott again. During our brief intercourse of one evening last winter, he had impressed me as manly, intelligent, and unaffected. But as he had then evidently chosen to regard me as just "one of the Marchmonts," whose name in New York is synonymous with extravagant fashion, there was only cool civility in his manner toward me; now he seemed surprised to hear that I was going to stop with Mrs. Wentworth.

"Dear Cousin Kate," he said with a scarcely disguised curl of the lip; "she has more strength and more weakness in her small body than any woman I know of. She is so absurdly good to all the world, and she has not the courage of her convictions to keep out of a society that she can not approve. You will see all there is to see of Bar Harbor gayety at Cousin Kate's cottage. She believes herself a hermit, whereas, in actual fact, she is in the centre of the social system. I used to stop with her myself. But I found that if I wanted rational enjoyment I must seek it elsewhere. Fancy putting on a long-tailed coat and varnished shoes, and wearing a high hat, at a Bar Harbor 'tea.' Yet that is what some of these latter-day decadents have come to. And the dinners are as numerous, as long, as conventional, as those at Newport. Believe me, you will feel quite at home."

Leaves from the Diary of Ruth Marchmont, Spinster

I was divided between my desire not to say another word to this scornful personage, and my curiosity to hear more.

"Putting me and my tastes quite out of the question," I answered, with self-control, "is it possible that there is a regularly organized system of fashionable life here? When I have heard people rave over it, I thought their delight was in the drives, and rides, and canoeing, the unrestraint of life being understood."

"Surely you are not old enough to remember the days when such an aboriginal state of things prevailed?" he said. "Long ago, when I came here as a boy, and later, in my college vacations, we went all day long in flannels, and concerned our-

Leaves from the Diary of Ruth Marchmont, Spinster

selves not a jot about conventions. But now — well, here we are, and, if I am so fortunate as to find you and my cousin Kate at home some day soon, you will tell me your impressions of the place."

The Wentworths were on the wharf to meet me, Kate charmingly dressed in a pink cotton that must have cost a fortune to make and trim as she had it. A French hat of pink chip with a forest of black feathers was upon her wise, kind, but over-busy little head. She led me through a crowd of people to a jaunty buckboard with a pair of ponies, and a man in "smart" livery to drive. While we whisked through the streets, I was surprised again to see shops like those at Newport, the sidewalk thronged with men and women in ultra-stylish costumes, the way encumbered with vehicles of the latest build; every evidence of gay society in full swing. Kate's whole time was taken up with nodding to people among whom I recognized many frequenters of our house in town.

"Oh! yes, the place is jammed," said my friend, when she could speak to me. "Sometimes I wish it were not so; but

Leaves from the Diary of Ruth Marchmont, Spinster

I've been here so long, I've a natural interest in seeing Bar Harbor come to the front. We always feel as if it is a brand snatched from the burning, when a Newport 'regular' comes here — and come they do, more every year, because it is more countrified, I suppose, all told, than Newport. And the air would put life into a moribund, as you will find. I don't know about its being cheaper here. The whole scale of things has gone up with every year of prosperity. And an enormous lot of money has gone into building great houses, and reclaiming wild land to make it as perfect as a park."

"I see nothing like a picnic," I exclaimed in disappointment. "These women sauntering along the plank-walk are all dressed in the most costly summer frocks — like yours, dear, pretty, but overdone."

"There speaks my Timon," said Kate, who is used to my sharp sayings. "I'll declare, Ruth, the only person who is crusty enough to match with you, is my cousin Hugh Elliott; and, as I live, there he is — stalking up the street to his old lodgings in that little village house."

Leaves from the Diary of Ruth Marchmont, Spinster

"We crossed the bay together," I said briefly. "But let us talk of this place. It looks to me as if I am not going to taste the flavor I have always heard is Bar Harbor's own especial charm."

"I beg your pardon," said Kate, who had turned aside to bow to a foreign diplomat driving a tandem dog-cart. "Look, Ruth, there are your sisters' friends, the Hamilton-Hookers, in that victoria. Their mother has taken a house here this summer, and is entertaining tremendously. We are due there, at a musicale, to-morrow afternoon, for which they have brought a string quartet from Boston, and a prima donna from New York. Then you are asked to a woman's luncheon at the Kebo Valley Club to-morrow, and I have some people coming to dinner in your honor to-morrow evening. On the chance that he might be in town, I sent a note asking Hugh Elliott also, but I doubt if he turns up."

A week later.

So much had I written when I laid down my pen; and, until to-day, I have not resumed it. I might begin again, by

Leaves from the Diary of Ruth Marchmont, Spinster

saying that Kate's intuition was perfectly correct. Mr. Elliott did not turn up at her dinner, but sent a very formal "regret," instead. I might never have seen him again, except that, two days later, I went out in the Wentworths' row-boat on a smooth sea, propelled by Kate's fourteen-year-old boy, who is a delightfully frank, sweet lad. I had taken the oars from him, and lost one of them, which floated away, leaving us rather absurdly helpless. Then a man in a canoe came along and recovered the oar, and brought it back to us. This hero proved to be Mr. Elliott, already browned by Mt. Desert suns and life in the open air. He lingered there beside us in the glowing evening light, amid that wonderful loveliness of landscape that makes one forget all social exuberances of the place in the joys nature confers at every turn. Without intending to do so, I said something to this effect, and Mr. Elliott responded in kind. We had a merry, jolly talk, in which Jack Wentworth took his full share, and it ended by our agreeing to go with Mr. Elliott the next day — I in his canoe, Jack in the boat — over to

Leaves from the Diary of Ruth Marchmont, Spinster

Sheep Porcupine, to spend the afternoon. Mr. Elliott appeared to much better advantage than I have ever seen him before.

Ten days later.

I don't know why it is so much harder to make regular entries in my diary here than in New York — or at Newport, even. One is so perpetually wooed away by charming effects of cloud upon the water, and by other things. Kate's house is like a *bonbonnière*, close to the water's edge, all white enamel paint inside, with soft-hued chintzes, and dainty bits of porcelain, and flower-boxes in every window — the prettiest place imaginable, and just suited to her Dresden china looks. I am all out of harmony with it in appearance, but she has given me a most bewitching bedroom that seems to hang over the water; and here, while Kate is away at her endless parties, I sit and gaze at the far hills upon the mainland; at the islands with their spikes of fir trees, scattered in the bay; at the glory of dawn and sunset; and ponder upon — other things!

Bar Harbor is better than I thought.

Part III

Leaves from the Diary of Ruth Marchmont, Spinster

Lenox, October, 189–.

AFTER the month of August spent at Bar Harbor with my friend Mrs. Wentworth in her charming cottage by the sea, I returned to join my father and brother at our farm in New Hampshire, where papa makes a pretence of breeding fine cattle, and potters about in a straw hat and old coat forgetting the fashionable existence into which he has been translated late in life by his ambitious wife and younger daughters. My brother John, who, to his mother's disgust, is a born farmer, really "runs" the place. I think he would like nothing better than to spend his days here, improving the forests around us, and looking after the crops and stock. Papa, who expects John to go into the business that was the foundation of all our wealth, has to be always reminding the poor dear boy that as soon as college days are over, he

Leaves from the Diary of Ruth Marchmont, Spinster

must "buckle down to work in the office, in town." I have once or twice remarked to my father, that, as rich as we are, we might surely let John follow out his own choice of life. But papa says, and perhaps with truth, he has no such sum of money accumulated as would suffice to support all his seven children in the style in which they have been brought up. "You are the only one of 'em, Ruthie," he says to me with a dry smile, "that, I think, could work for a living, if necessity compelled you to do so. You remind me of my own mother, child; she was one of the lean kine, like you, and never knew when to leave off work."

Late in September, I was obliged to go down to Newport, and look into the affairs of the family of care-takers who, during my mother's absence in Europe, had been left in charge of what the newspapers called the "Marchmont palace." It seems that burglars, arrested on the premises, proved to be near relations of these estimable guardians of our home. It was therefore necessary to turn them out, and install others. My father, easy going, and not inclined to exertion, accepted my offer to attend to the whole matter. I spent a day in solitary majesty in the great, splendid, shut-up house, and then my dear friend and co-worker in many charities, Mrs. Gramercy, of New York, came and carried me off to pass the remainder of the week with her in her Newport cottage.

Leaves from the Diary of Ruth Marchmont, Spinster

In Agatha Gramercy's company I always feel at my best. She is eager, alert, full of high aims and impossible fancies like myself, but infinitely more pleasing and pliant and winning to outsiders in her way of expressing these ideas. She softens my asperity of temper; she encourages me to believe there is something worth living for in the circle of society we both belong to; and, at her house, one is always sure of meeting *live* people.

At the end of the week nothing would suffice Agatha but that I should accompany her on a visit to her mother, who has a house at Lenox. That accounts for the heading of this entry in my diary. When I left the farm, I had no idea of doing anything but return there to await the

Leaves from the Diary of Ruth Marchmont, Spinster

arrival of my mother and sisters in New York in mid-October.

There has been a change in their plans also. Martha, the older of the two girls, has become engaged to young Sir Willoughby Caton, a baronet who has one or two beautiful houses in England, and spends his time on the Continent because he cannot afford to keep up his ancestral homes. Mama had written to my father at length about the prospect of a proposal from Sir Willoughby at the German spa where they were all stopping. When the proposal came, there was nothing for her to do, therefore, but cable for papa's consent. As if he, poor dear, had ever ventured to go contrary to mama and Martha and Elizabeth. So he obediently cabled back his acquiescence, and as he says, "the ladies" will soon be in Paris buying the trousseau. The wedding is to occur in New York in November, and Martha will at once sail for her new home. She seems to be enchanted with her prospects. How much of it is love for the man, how much excitement over her title, her trousseau, the new tiara papa is to be made to give

Leaves from the Diary of Ruth Marchmont, Spinster

her, and all the rest of it, I can't make out. One thing is certain. Sir Willoughby is the "real thing," in the matter of position, or Martha would not have taken him. She is as level-headed a young woman as she is beautiful and distinguished in appearance. Papa will give her a liberal portion, and what will become of Elizabeth unless she, too, captures a title, I do not know. Those girls have always seemed to think there is nobody in their own country who can offer what they merit in point of lofty place.

How different it is with me. I—but then, I shall never marry. The few who have sought me have wanted papa's daughter, and papa's daughter's *dot*. He whom I would—no, I shall certainly never marry. It is not upon the cards.

We have come to Lenox in its loveliest season of the year. The rolling hill country is full of delightful variety to the eye. We go out every day for long drives, over breezy uplands, down into verdant hollows where lie jewel-bright lakes, between hills clothed with wonderful masses of forest foliage, just now radiant in tints I cannot

Leaves from the Diary of Ruth Marchmont, Spinster

describe. Some of the views from the verandas of this house where I am staying are like Turner's best canvases in point of rich, soft, luminous color. I do not wonder that wealthy, leisurely folk come here to linger away from New York and Boston until nearly Christmas-time. The air of the place, the houses, and the entertainments are more quiet and mellow than anything in Newport or Bar Harbor. There does not seem to be the strain in living here. The inevitable dinners and luncheons go on just as in the other resorts I have named, but one comes in to dress for them after rides and drives into the very fastnesses of Nature, through shady, moss-carpeted woods amid a rain of tinted leaves, or upon good roads high among the hills looking over miles of peaceful rural country. This daily attrition with Nature is restful and refreshing, and, after it, to "look in" as Agatha calls it, at the pretty houses with the pleasant people around their tea-tables and luncheon tables, is not a bad experience. Perhaps Agatha's companionship is the secret of my contentment here. And then, neither she nor her dear old mother, Mrs. Weldon, pushes one to enjoy one's self. There is never, at their breakfast table, a breathless review of the engagements for the day. They never go anywhere in the morning hours, unless to walk into the village. Every guest seeks his or her own diversion, and is unchallenged by the hostess. Agatha, like me, will not accept an invitation to a set luncheon, which she declares unfits one for healthy exertion during the rest of the afternoon and evening. To repeat such a meal at dinner, a few hours later, is beyond normal capacity, and no doubt accounts for the "too solid flesh" under which many of our American matrons are groaning. In England, no matter how great the establishment, luncheon is a simple meal, with at most a couple of hot dishes; and people take what they prefer — are not served with each dish in turn at their elbows. At some houses in Lenox this same agreeable fashion prevails, and the Weldons' is of that kind. Another nice thing about Lenox is the habit of resorting to sit out upon velvet

Leaves from the Diary of Ruth Marchmont, Spinster

Leaves from the Diary of Ruth Marchmont, Spinster

lawns, to look on at tennis or archery. There is more land enclosed here, for purposes of pleasure, around the houses, than in most places of summer resort I know; and I dare say that, after all, is what gives Lenox its air of undeniable good-breeding and reserve.

Having written so much in favor of Lenox, I go back with a sudden exhilaration of spirit to the memory of Bar Harbor. Certain brilliant mornings out-of-doors there, in the saddle among the woods of pine and birch, — certain afternoons in boat or canoe cutting the tranquil bosom of the bay, or riding the swell of the long Atlantic waves off the seaward coast of the island, — rise up before me with irresistible power. I think I had rather repeat these experiences than do anything else in the world; and I have knowledge of a great many other choice places in the world.

Ah me! — I have written that down because I found myself actually saying it aloud. I ruffle the leaves of this book, and subsequent to a certain day in August, I find no mention of Bar Harbor. Over

and again, I have tried to put into black
and white emotions felt there during that
month, and have failed to do so. I can
hardly believe it is cool, self-contained,
indifferent Ruth Marchmont, who has
spent years of her life analyzing the
springs of action and feeling among those
around her, who dares not trust herself to
revert to an experience in which the chief
part was played by a man who could go
off and leave her without an expression
of regret!

Leaves from the Diary of Ruth Marchmont, Spinster

During four weeks at Bar Harbor, in
August, I saw Hugh Elliott almost every
day. From casual and rather antagonistic
acquaintance, we passed into a sympathy
of mind and feeling that is unique in my
experience. All this, be it understood,
without a hint of the relation between
man and girl that generally takes on a sentimental complexion, and ends by wrecking
what might otherwise have been an ideal
friendship. But I was doomed to a disappointment in him, that has left me sore
indeed. One afternoon he called and left
two cards, — two miserable little conventional visiting cards, — one for my hostess,

Leaves from the Diary of Ruth Marchmont, Spinster

the other for me. The next day we heard that he had left Bar Harbor. From that day to this, I have never had a word, good, bad, or indifferent, to show that he remembers my existence.

The above, as usual, was penned after I went to my room at night. After writing the last word, I heard a tap at my door, and Agatha, in her trailing *robe de chambre*, of pearl color with rosy linings, came in. "I thought I should find you scribbling," she said; "but I want a few words with you before you go to sleep. I've had a letter I want to consult you about. You know my husband has a tremendous friendship with Hugh Elliott." I started like a school-girl in love, but Agatha did not appear to notice me. "I wonder if I ever told you, dear, what a splendid fellow we think Hugh is. The 'man of the future,' I always call him. And when you and I set our ideal society in order, he will occupy a high place in it. Well born, more than well educated, strong, and self-reliant, an American of the best type, I had in my heart, associated him, without knowing why, with you.

Yet I could never get him to meet you. He had a rooted objection to your 'class' in society; and I am too proud of you, Ruth, to vaunt your attractions in such a way. Why did you never tell me he met you last summer at Bar Harbor; that he fell in love as fervently and earnestly as it is possible for a man to do; that he left you abruptly because he feared to trust himself with a girl between whom and himself there is such disparity of fortune. Lately something very nice has happened to him,—an advance in place; a man as clever as he was bound to get ahead, and he is now sure. As it happened, mama had invited him to come to-morrow for a 'Saturday-to-Monday,' and he accepts, without knowing you are here. Now, Ruth, I think too much of both of you, to let him come, if—"

Leaves from the Diary of Ruth Marchmont, Spinster

"If what, Agatha," I said quite helplessly, not knowing the sound of my own voice.

"Oh! Ruth, dear, as if I do not know you better than you do yourself. What is it that has so altered you of late?"

"Agatha, if you do, I shall never for-

Leaves from the Diary of Ruth Marchmont, Spinster

give you as long as I live," I exclaimed unmeaningly, and then cried; and so did she. And we kissed each other fondly, as I am afraid the strong ideal women of our future dreamland never will do.

Sunday night.

I have been sitting out on the veranda with Mr. Elliott. The stars shone bright, and the air, soft as midsummer, was laden with the delicious scents of autumn.

He says we shall work out together my dream of a higher life.

Thirteen at Table

Thirteen at Table

IF any one had told Felicia Charlton, the year before, that she would be spending this summer at Newport as a dweller in one of the most famous of the new houses that are the glory of that favored resort, she would have laughed in the face of the recounter of such a fairy-tale,— that merry heartsome laugh of hers,— for Felicia well deserved her name.

But the event least expected had occurred. The gay, pretty, poverty-stricken Southern girl, the daughter of an ancient line; who during her nineteen years of life had never known any but the hard rubs of fortune; who had grown up to womanhood under the wing of a widowed mother scarce eighteen years her senior, as lovely to look at as is Felicia herself, but for the traces left on her face and form by care and by thought how to make a subsistence for the two and to provide an education for Felicia that should enable her to be self-supporting.

Latterly things had gone from bad to worse with the Charltons. They had spent one year in the desolation of a poor country neighborhood with relatives glad of the pittance their board afforded; and at the end of it, Mrs. Charlton had accepted an offer from a friend of early days who was about to open a boarding-school, to act as her housekeeper. At the same time, Felicia entered upon the exhilarating career of assistant to a decayed gentlewoman in Baltimore, who made and sold the pickles and preserves so renowned in old-time Maryland cook-books. And all this while the girl's high spirits had never flagged. She had laughed and prattled, and won smiles from the little mother in her hours of darkest despondency. She had even coaxed into moments of cheerfulness the broken-spirited lady who manufactured pickles and preserves; and, while carrying on her uncongenial work, lost no opportunity of looking for something better. In this stress, to Felicia's credit be it inscribed, it did not occur to her to write verses, or a story, and send them to a first-class magazine.

Summer had come around again, and the prospect of spending it in a piping hot flat, in the temperature of Baltimore, between June and October, and in the company of Mrs. Ballantyne and her gas stove, was all that presented itself to Felicia's mental gaze. But in her heart a little bird kept singing, over and over, the blithe tidings that her mother's employer was to take her old friend on a visit of two months to the mountains of Virginia, where Miss Kennard was wont to return in her vacations to the household of parents who could give her food and drink and a shelter, at least. How much better was this than Felicia had dared to hope! Fresh air, fresh milk, shade trees on a green lawn, the Blue Ridge Mountains encompassing their daily horizon, — what matter if the poor old plantation house were falling to rack and ruin, so that there was a roof to cover Felicia's dear little mother, to whom all these luxuries were promised by Miss Kennard.

It had not been without a fierce maternal struggle in the little widow's breast, that this invitation had been accepted. That she should be taken, and Felicia left, cost her gentle heart strange pangs. But Felicia, who had a way with her none could withstand, had simply forced her point. She had packed her mother's trunk, had gone with her to the station, had parted with her to all appearance joyfully, and then, to save car-fare, had set out to walk over the burning bricks of the pavement, on her return to Mrs. Ballantyne's.

Just then, a little victoria had driven close to the sidewalk near her, and pulled up. A young woman charmingly dressed had leaned forward and hailed her by name. Felicia with a start of pleasant surprise recognized an old schoolmate, a western heiress who had recently married and taken up her abode here in her husband's city.

Between the two girls had passed the usual expressions of fervent greeting, and Felicia, promptly installed under the hood of the victoria, was quickly on the way with Mrs. Branham to her pretty bridal home.

What a contrast to it was presented by the dull and paltry sitting-room of Mrs. Ballantyne's flat, where, later, whilst adjusting their modest tea-table, Felicia tried to entertain her employer with her new budget of gossip. But the dame, who had a touch of toothache, and was not much in sympathy with the holiday side of life of which so little had fallen to her share, responded sparely, and Felicia, after washing the tea-things, had retired to the back window to get a breath of air while meditating upon the exciting incidents of the day.

More than on anything Maud Branham had shown her, Felicia dwelt upon a hint Maud had let fall of helping her to better her fortunes.

"I have a cousin, Mrs. Dwight Caldwell, who goes to Newport every summer from New York," the bride observed; "and I think, though I am not sure, I heard her say she wishes to engage a secretary to take there with her this year. I can easily ask, Felicia; and I'm sure, if you got it, you'd be in luck. Such a splendid establishment hers is,—this of mine would be swallowed up in it,—and they entertain everybody and go everywhere. She is one of the people one reads about in the society columns of the Sunday newspapers. Her husband is a nice fellow, but he spends most of his time at the club. Sally Caldwell certainly goes at full speed in society, but she has always been a good-natured thing when I've seen her, and I don't doubt you'd be good friends. I shall write this very night and ask Sally; and how awfully jolly it will be if I succeed!"

Felicia, in her calmer mood, recalling Maud at school as a kind, chattering, but somewhat dense creature, had a moment's hesitation about trusting to the judgment of her friend. But all night long her dreams were roseate. A situation as secretary with a salary that she could lay by for her mother's use next winter! As friend and patron, a brilliant cultured woman of the world who would inspire in her a thousand new ideas, as well as open the door for her into a wonder world of luxurious beauty! Above all, opportunity to see something beyond her accustomed horizon, to breathe a fresh delicious atmosphere, to see everywhere sights of refined loveliness! Oh! it was too good to be true.

A few days later, a note arrived from Maud Branham asking Felicia to luncheon the next day; and when Felicia presented herself as desired, no time was lost by the good-natured young matron in communicating her great news. Sally Caldwell was already at Newport; Sally Caldwell had just sent away a girl she had taken there who turned out to be absurdly stupid and inefficient, and saucy, too; and Sally Caldwell was prepared to accept Maud's friend upon Maud's recommendation, provided she would "come right away," naming a salary that seemed to Felicia's limited experience a king's ransom in amount.

The girl's head swam; a mist came before her eyes. When she recovered her self-possession enough to speak, it was, woman-like, to ask Maud's advice about the clothes she possessed, and the clothes she would require. Maud, also a true daughter of Eve, was here quite in her element. Not only did she generously offer to lend Felicia money for her journey, but, after luncheon, took her to her room, and there produced two or three frocks and jackets and bonnets of which Felicia was requested to make her choice.

"For you know, dear, if I have a weakness, it is for always buying something in the latest fashion, and disliking it when bought. It is ridiculous, the things I have stored away that I can never use, and that never would suit me anyhow. If you can't take these as a present from an old friend and schoolmate, why, I shall never speak to you again as long as I live."

Felicia's laugh rang out. Here was Maud's old familiar threat of schooldays. Just now, she seemed to be an irresistible fairy-godmother, who had only to wave her stick to be obeyed.

Mrs. Charlton, in her remote Virginia refuge, had read her darling's first letter from Newport with almost ecstatic pride and joy. It seemed to the poor lady that no one had ever been blessed with such a lovely and loving and clever and successful daughter as was she. After she had perused the epistle for the second time, she took it out upon what old Mrs. Kennard called the "front poache." This was a rickety veranda over which grew a vine of custard honeysuckle; and here old Mr. Kennard sat, tilted upon his chair, under a shelf supporting the water bucket and a gourd, conning a weekly newspaper. Near at hand, sitting also in a split-bottom chair, with her knitting, the old lady listened with admiration to the occasional oracles of information transmitted to her from the columns before him through her husband's eyes. After long practise in receiving her news and literature thus at second hand, she had grown to esteem him personally responsible for the well-rounded sentences. Coming around the corner of the house, Miss Kennard, in a sunbonnet, was seen carrying in a wooden bowl a brood of motherless chicks. Upon the threshold of the door, and on both steps of the porch, dogs were dozing. "How trivial everything else will seem," thought the little widow, advancing proudly among them with her letter, "when they hear what my child thinks of Newport."

Whilst these things were occurring in far tranquil Virginia, Felicia was looking daily upon the passing show of Newport. What a thrilling effect upon her imagination had been created by the first view of the sumptuous part of the town, as she approached it in the little trap that had been sent to meet her on arrival. It happened to be at an hour when the gay world was on wheels; and while our little girl was gazing with all her eyes upon the kaleidoscope of vehicles and people, she observed the groom, who was driving her, touch his hat to a handsome, haughty lady, whose gaze just then fell upon them from her victoria. Felicia saw that she was the object of this lady's thorough and perfectly frigid scrutiny — and, to her surprise, became aware that the survey was followed by an infinitesimal nod in her direction.

When the carriages had passed each

other, the groom, leaning back, said in rather too jocular a fashion for Felicia's sense of propriety:

"That's her. That's the madam, goin' out for her drive."

Felicia, answering him with a cold look, asked no questions. The incident, occurring upon the threshold of her new experience, struck her unpleasantly. With her simple, hearty, Southern ideas, she could not imagine arrival in a strange house without some sort of a personal welcome from the hostess; and the quality of that investigating gaze was to her totally unknown. But, taking heart, she noted with delight the exquisite beauty of the verdant lawns and radiant flower-beds on either side the well-kept driveway leading up to such a house as surpassed her fondest dream of imposing completeness. The striped yellow awnings over all the windows on the front, shading flower boxes that overflowed with bloom; the verandas yielding glimpses of chairs and couches and tall palms; and, above all, the flowers and plants massed in every angle where they could be placed in exterior decoration, seemed to Felicia incredibly enchanting. As she sprang out of the trap and looked around her, catching a distant vista of blue sea at the end of a reach of velvet sward, she was dazed with excitement. She forgot that she had been left standing there alone; and her first fall from the clouds was caused by the too easy manner and language of a lady's maid who came to escort her to her room.

Felicia had nothing to complain of in externals, certainly. The room that was assigned to her, all white-and-rose and green-stained furniture with a window looking upon the sea, was delightfully cool and tempting. Tea was served to her there; her little trunk was brought in and unstrapped; and upon the table she found a book or two, should she wish to pass her time otherwise than by looking out of the flower-framed shaded window. But, by and by, a sense of loneliness set in; and, to banish it, she stole out for a walk about the grounds.

Gazing from a shaded bench upon the cliff over the sea, an infinite peace fell upon her spirit. How long she had sat there she did not know, until she became conscious that a young man in summer flannels had come along the path leading to her eyrie, and was searching for something he had lost.

"I beg your pardon," he said, taking off his hat; "I did not know any one had succeeded me in my favorite haunt."

"You are looking for this?" she said, holding out a little compass of gold and crystal she had picked up, then forgotten.

"Yes, thank you. It represents the economies of my small sister, who sent it to me for a birthday gift to-day," he said, taking the trifle from her finger tips. "I suppose you have just come, and have not yet seen our hostess."

Cheered by his cordial tone, Felicia answered as girls of her race and bringing-up are wont to do; easily, fearlessly, smiles playing around her rosy lips and in her friendly eyes; and, at once, they were launched upon a conversation that proved, apparently, as satisfactory to Duncan Moore as it certainly was to our poor little confiding Felicia, tongue-tied for so many hours and aching to communicate her sensations to somebody.

She at once discovered that Mr. Moore was, like herself, an inmate of the house; was spending a fortnight with the Caldwells, and was already almost "done to death" with the insistence of Newport hospitality. He, of course, took this artless and refreshing little person, whose good looks charmed his eye, to be a guest upon his own plane. Even if Felicia had suspected his mistake, it would not have occurred to her to do more than laugh at it. "Down South," the young lady engaged to be governess or companion or secretary is in all things a member of the family; and when, as usual, she is well born and well bred, the fact of poverty is the merest bagatelle, so far as social consideration is concerned. How could it enter into Felicia's head that she was henceforth to be taboo to the familiar associates of her employer?

Luckily, upon this occasion, she was spared finding it out. The maidenly reserve that in her underlaid a manner almost coquettish in its directness, prompted her to withdraw from the interview. As she arose, and Moore offered to walk to the house with her, with the prettiest gesture of a small white hand she motioned him to remain —

"But why?" he said, "or, at least, when shall I talk with you again?"

"When you shall have been properly introduced," she replied, vanishing from his sight.

Moore sat for a while upon the forsaken bench, till shadows lengthening upon the lawn, and the purple light of evening on the sea, sent him within doors to dress for dinner. When he came down into the library where the house-party met before dinner was announced, he looked eagerly about him, but in the various groups saw no sign of the fairy of the cliff. As luck would have it, his seat at table that night was far away from Mrs. Caldwell's and, until just after the men came in from the smoke-room, he had no opportunity to make inquiries of his hostess.

"The young lady who arrived this afternoon?" repeated Mrs. Caldwell in bewilderment. "You are dreaming. Nobody new is here. You know they say I am faithful to the same old gang; and you are all present, I believe."

Moore shrank a little from her, as he went on in his dogged way.

"Miss Charlton, I mean. The young lady from Virginia, who came while you were driving."

Mrs. Caldwell threw back her dark, well-coifed head, with a peal of laughter.

"I see what you mean now. It's my new secretary who's come to replace that dreadful pushing creature I told you of; and, if you believe me, I got in so late to dress, I have not seen her yet. How could you make such a mistake?"

"What mistake?"

"To—er—suppose that she was one of my guests?"

Moore, angered by her supercilious drawl, felt his color rise. Then restraining himself, he turned on his heel and left her, inwardly resolving not to spend another day under the roof of this pretentious worldling.

But when the next day came, he did not go away.

Poor Felicia! It was all such a sad awakening. Twenty-four hours spent in her new capacity were quite sufficient to show her that business, not friendship, was the platform on which she stood. Mrs. Caldwell, when, on the morning following her arrival, she summoned her latest employée into the dainty boudoir where Felicia's duties were to be performed, had received her with the most perfunctory of handshakes, and without a smile. The girl, unaccustomed to this omission of social courtesies, fancied herself an offender, and for a moment stood sick at heart with wondering what she had done. In a short time, however, Mrs. Caldwell made it perfectly clear that Miss Charlton had in no wise transgressed, and was even welcome in the stress of her employer's arrears of correspondence. Leaning back in a deep wicker chair with fantastic frilled cushions of China silk, beside a table filled with specimen vases of emerald glass, each containing a perfect rose, the great lady dictated a dozen little notes of courtesy, conventionality, or charity, which Felicia's fleet pen transcribed upon sheets from a

Thirteen at Table silver-mounted paper-case upon a table littered with every contrivance for elegant dalliance with letters. This done, and evidently done to Mrs. Caldwell's satisfaction, Felicia received instructions to fill up a series of dinner-invitations, with names and dates, for a banquet to be given three weeks off; and to address envelopes from a list furnished her, for a musicale for which a great artist had been engaged to come up from New York.

"This will give you enough for to-day," said Mrs. Caldwell, rising to go. "You will consider this room your own to sit in at all hours, but your meals will be taken in what we call the school-room, which is more convenient for the servants to carry the trays into. I — er — think you probably dined there last night. It is a nice little room, and I hope you will take care that they give you everything nicely. The housekeeper has the strictest orders about my secretary's comfort, and you must immediately report to her if anything is omitted. At any time when you want to drive out, one of the grooms can take you in the basket phaeton; and, as you see, there are books here — and a piano, if you play. I am happy to say that I think you will suit me exactly; and I am glad Maud Branham spoke of you. Your salary will be paid monthly, and here (handing her a cheque) is the first month in advance, as you may have some purchases to make."

This was a kindly thought, and to it Felicia's spirit responded; but, looking into Mrs. Caldwell's ever-unsmiling face, she dared not speak. The lady rustled from the room, and Felicia, left alone in the apartment that was so far beyond her dreams of luxury, dropped her little head down upon the blotter before her, and burst into tears.

"She does not mean to be unkind," Felicia mused, after a week of her new life had passed. "I think, in her heart, she fancies she is a model patroness. But oh! the way I am made to feel my distance! Never a laugh or a jest for me; yet as soon as she rejoins any of her guests, she is the gayest of the gay. She must know — Maud told her — I am a lady born, and entitled to rank with the best. I wonder if it ever occurred to her what life is without anybody to talk to, or to confide in. I suppose a really superior character would find solace in this beautiful room and the walks and drives and, above all, in books. But I never said I am a superior character. I want people, people, people. Somebody to sympathize with me; somebody to hear my chatter. How many things I've noticed here in Newport, that it would be such fun to talk over. I'll declare I almost hate this lovely old-blue wall-paper, and the white enamelled furniture, and the blue china ornaments, and that heavenly bit of blue glimmering sea over the flower-box in the window. I know, now, how a canary must feel in his cage. I want to get out. I want to sing, to spread my wings outside."

As Felicia spoke, the dimples came back into her cheeks; her eyes shone blue as the sea; she sprang from her seat, and, pushing away the chairs from a space on the mirror-like parquetted floor, began to tread the measure of a solitary minuet.

After Mrs. Caldwell had left her for the morning, she was sure of several uninterrupted hours; and now she must relieve her restlessness or perish, the little maiden thought. So, humming the minuet from "Don Giovanni," she accompanied it by footsteps light as thistle down. Nearing the door into the hall, she did not perceive it was ajar, until a tap came, and at the aperture was revealed to her startled view a gentleman.

"Oh!" exclaimed Felicia, instantly transformed into a statue of confusion.

"I don't know what you think of me bolting in like this," said Mr. Duncan Moore, penitentially. "But Mrs. Caldwell is responsible. She is just about starting for her round of visits, and told me to run up and get her address book — that is, she told her footman Miss Charlton would give it to him, and as he did not hear her, I came. I hope you won't mind. I've been wanting awfully to see you, ever since that day, and to ask you to take a walk with me; but, somehow, I couldn't get a chance. Why do they keep you mewed up like this? It is shameful to treat you as if you were fifty and a frump."

"Here is the book," said Felicia, putting into his hands a silver-clasped affair of lizard skin. "You need not apologize, I am not angry. I am only too thankful to speak to somebody who is not a servant."

"Thanks for small favors," he replied rather nettled.

"But I am very much ashamed that you saw me prancing about like a lunatic," she went on; "I was only taking a little exercise, and now, please go, for Mrs. Caldwell does not like to be kept waiting."

"Will you fix an hour to walk with me?" he pursued eagerly.

"No, I can't; so don't mention it again."

"Will you talk to me somewhere — anywhere?"

"How can I?" asked Felicia, ready to cry, because in her heart she should have liked nothing better than the companionship of this hearty, bright-faced young fellow.

"Then I shall just go out of this house

to-morrow," he said, like a spoiled child. "As if I hadn't stayed on here a week, for nothing but to get another peep at you."

"Don't, please," said Felicia, now earnestly; and with an impatient gesture he departed.

That evening one of Mrs. Caldwell's periodical dinners, for which the invitations had long been sent out and accepted, was to take place. Felicia, who was by now used to such things at secondhand, when sent down to give the butler the dinner cards and the chart of the seats, had lingered, looking on at the glittering table with its burden of silver and waxlights, and banks of maidenhair and roses. She was no longer so much impressed with mere externals as at first. Grandeur, viewed from afar, had begun to pall on her. But she had quaint, wistful imaginings of what it would be to be led in to table by such a man as Duncan Moore, for example, and sit there as a part of it. In this crisis of her rash fancies, Hortense, Mrs. Caldwell's maid, came in search of her.

Thirteen at Table "Hurry, mademoiselle," said Hortense, with a touch of authority. "Madame must see you immediately, *dans sa chambre*."

Madame, in her teagown, sat before her mirror, the picture of perplexity, an open note in her hand.

"Can you imagine anything more vexatious?" she exclaimed pathetically. "Miss Clayton has a headache, and cannot come. That girl is spoiled beyond all endurance by being set up as the season's beauty; and I don't believe in her headache in the least. I have racked my brain to think of some one to replace her, and failed. I should not mind, but Mrs. Mammon, who thinks it such a tremendous condescension if she comes to you at all, will not dine thirteen on any account. She would not hesitate to call for her carriage and go home, if she found out we were thirteen. There's no help for it, Miss Charlton, you *must* come down and fill the vacant place. Dress is, I suppose, your difficulty, but Hortense is invaluable in suggestion for such an emergency. In all my things she can surely find something you can wear."

Felicia wanted to rebel against the whole of the programme; but against the latter part of it, she did rebel.

"I have a pale-blue crepon that is very nice," she said quietly. "It has a low bodice trimmed with a fall of just such old Malines lace as you have on your pearl color, but finer. It was my mother's lace," she added, seeing Hortense stare. "If I may wear that, Mrs. Caldwell, to oblige you I will come down."

"Certainly, certainly," cried the relieved lady, breathing freer. "I — er — suppose you won't wear ornaments, Miss Charlton."

"Don't be afraid of that," exclaimed the girl lightly, and then ran off to her room.

Resentful of her enforced position, she glided down stairs just as the guests were falling into line to go into the dining-room. From the shadow under the stairway, she was intercepted and captured by Duncan Moore.

"I am actually, and without solicitation, to take you in to dinner," he said, offering her his hand. I have been looking for you ever since Mrs. Caldwell gave me notice of my good luck."

He did not tell her the notice was accompanied by profuse apologies at imposing this service upon a "very good friend." In his heart, he rejoiced at escaping that conceited Irene Clayton who could think and speak of nothing but her own successes in the social world of Newport. And, as the dinner progressed, he observed, with considerable satisfaction, that many approving glances were cast by the other men present upon his charming little partner. For Felicia, forgetting her woes, arose to the occasion royally. Her color deepened; her eyes grew starry; her animation was irresistible to look upon and to share in. The man on her other side, a maker of opinion in Newport, even turned his back upon the conversation of Mrs. Mammon to enjoy this delightfully fresh and sparkling little new girl whom Mrs. Caldwell had been so clever as to discover.

From exultant satisfaction, Mr. Duncan Moore retired more than once into the sulks, when he found her attention as freely bestowed upon her other neighbor as upon himself; then, each time that Felicia returned to him, he was renewed in hope.

It does not require as much time for Cupid, sly wight, to wing a shaft into a young man's bosom that will rankle there for all time, as for me to write this sentence.

Already Duncan Moore, whose desirableness as a *parti* did not in the least affect Felicia, vowed to himself that if he could not win this young woman to be his, he would not look at any other. It may be added that it was in consequence of a falling out with him, whom Miss Clayton had believed to be her own possession, that the young lady had failed to be present at the dinner which afforded him his chance at her rival.

"How very, very good of you," murmured Mrs. Caldwell to Mr. Moore, when the men came out from dinner.

"Yes," said Mrs. Mammon; "and as I understand it was all for my sake, I appreciate it the more."

"Where is that charming Miss Charlton?" asked Mr. Trent, who had sat upon Felicia's right at table. "How one does enjoy those little Southern thoroughbreds, when they are both pretty and merry, as she is! You are a clever woman, Mrs. Caldwell, to get such attractions for your feast."

Moore, who had responded to neither lady's speech, stood glaring into the corners of the great dusky drawing-room with its pink shaded lamps, as if in search of her.

"I think it likely my secretary has gone to her own room," said Mrs. Caldwell to Mr. Trent. "I was just confessing to Mrs. Mammon that I had her in to play the *quatorzième* on a pinch."

Moore — who saw what had happened, that poor little Felicia, like many another of her sex before her, left alone among the women, had been driven from the field — felt a sudden desire to champion the oppressed before the world, to which he did not, at first, exactly see his way to give expression, without transgressing propriety.

"You are really very civil," said his hostess with a short laugh. "Why should you look like a thunder-cloud because Miss Charlton has shown the good sense to go back to her proper place? One would think that, with you, instead of being *quatorzième*, this young person is *première*," and she laughed again, meaningly.

This gave Moore his opportunity. "She is not, but shall be, if you are going to be kind enough to give me your help to win her," he said, where she alone could hear him. Mrs. Caldwell, who had begun to laugh as if this were a capital joke, was silenced by the earnest expression of the young man's eyes. And then, by one of those caprices of nature, who delights in the development of unexpected traits, the woman's heart inside of her crust of worldliness was touched.

"Good gracious, I believe you mean it!" she exclaimed, wondering.

"I do mean it," he answered seriously.

"To tell the truth, I have found nothing but good in her," went on the lady; "and now, I think she is lucky as well as good."

Thirteen at Table   Thus Felicia's episode as a bread-winner in the circles of high society was shortened in the fashion varied, but substantially the same, from age to age.

At a Winter House-Party

At a Winter House-Party

IT was pleasant tidings to all concerned, that a woman of fashion and consequence, yclept by her friends Mrs. "Algy" Bliss, had taken it into her good-natured head to open a big house she owned in the hill country some hours out of town, warm it to summer heat, stock it with cates and comforts, servants and recent magazines, and ask twenty people to come there for a mid-winter house-party.

The season of gayeties in town had just reached the happy point when the healthy boys and girls of this athletic generation, who are its chief supporters, felt themselves overdone with artificial pleasures. To most of them, the real entertainment of life consists not of dancing,—that *fâde* resource of outworn society,—but of golf, bicycling, riding, tobogganing, and the like, so that the prospect of a "Friday-to-Monday" out-of-doors was almost a requital

At a Winter House-Party

for what they had undergone in the way of dinners, the opera, and balls. As for the semi-occasional chaperon included in Mrs. Algy's invitations, she could look forward to an oasis of good food and good company; with leave to go to bed early in the soothing silence of a wide amphitheatre of hills, and to wake up late with no sound of vehicles rattling upon a stony street to distress her nerves.

Mrs. Algy's hospitality was therefore rewarded by unanimous acceptance and prompt appearance at the tryst. Twenty-four hours of fun and frolic with Dame Nature in winter livery, had put everybody in the very best of spirits. They had come down for a skating contest upon a pretty sheet of crystal girdled with tall woods and cheered by two mighty bonfires on the shore, that sent billowing smoke-wreaths high toward the heavens already streaked with the crimson of the sunset.

The point of meeting and departure for the skaters was a rustic tea-house, near the edge of the lake, fitted inside with a picturesque jumble of Eastern draperies and screens and studio "effects" in general.

At a Winter House-Party

In a massive fireplace constructed of rocks, to which still clung the moss and lichens of the woods, a fire of logs of hickory was burning. Before it was spread a Turkish rug, and on this little island of gay color appeared a tea-table, presided over by Mrs. Algy herself, well wrapped in becoming furs. Upon the good lady's handsome face was seen no mark of care surpassing her anxiety that everybody should have the right number of lumps of sugar in her tea. A pair of admirable footmen, moving about with cups, seemed to have been expressly provided by Heaven to forestall Mrs. Algy's needs.

Standing by her hostess, one slender foot on the low, wrought-iron fender, was a tall, distinguished-looking girl, with rather weary large blue eyes. One could see at a glance that she had been "out" for several seasons, and had not yet done with theories.

In a wicker-chair drawn up to get the best part of the blaze sat a lady, also unmarried, no longer young, not pretty, but possessed of a certain decorative quality in attire. Miss Brenton was desirable to

At a Winter House-Party

hostesses, in that she was passed along their line, burdened with the most recent budget of infinite nothings concerning the only people really worth hearing about — the members of their own set. At the present moment, while apparently stirring her tea, she was actually engaged in watching the effect upon her former schoolmate, Gwendolyn Talcott, of a speech she had thought well enough of to reiterate.

"Yes, I had it — if not exactly in so many words — from the girl's own mother to-day. Pray how does it strike you, Gwendolyn?"

"How does any announcement of a new engagement strike any one? A little wonder, a little babble, and the thing glides down the stream," said Miss Talcott, taking her foot from the fender, and beginning to pull on her jacket to go out.

"Let me help you with your sleeves, dear," exclaimed Miss Brenton, jumping up to face Gwendolyn, as she effusively performed the proffered service.

"Isn't she rather young for him?" asked Mrs. Algy, who was never too much surprised by anything.

At a Winter House-Party

"Young?" exclaimed Miss Brenton, her eyes fixed upon Gwendolyn's face, while hovering officiously about her. "Bless me, dear Mrs. Bliss, do you forget that for a man, time stands still between thirty and forty — and Brook isn't more than thirty-two! It's a dreadfully unfair distribution of things; for here, Gwendolyn and I, at twenty-six, are already 'old girls.' All the younger set call us 'Miss,' and get up and offer us seats when we come into the room. Besides, a man like Brook, who has seen everything, needs, when he marries, to be refreshed, amused, looked up to as an oracle. He doesn't want a mature being with a mission, behind his coffee-urn, but a little pink and white Dresden shepherdess, like Gracie. Lucky Brook! He can be choosing still, while Gwen and I must wait to be picked up and thank the picker — eh! Gwendolyn?"

Miss Talcott made no reply, but Mrs. Algy supplied the deficiency. She was conscious of a faint discomfort that even the admirable footmen could not remove.

"Then that accounts for it. My husband wired me this morning, that Brook

At a Winter House-Party

would probably come up with him this afternoon, to stay over Sunday. And here I was wondering why he was so sociable all at once, when he has never before accepted one of my invitations. I think Mrs. Wotherspoon might have given a hint of this first to me, instead of to you, Josephine. She said it was neuralgia that kept her at the house this afternoon."

"Don't be severe on her, dear," said Josephine Brenton, nimbly. "Think what a rise for the Wotherspoons to intermarry with the Brooks."

"Gracie is my Clara's age," pursued the matron, "and I should never have thought of Clara and Mr. Brook together. The child is pretty, of course, for any one who admires that excessively fair hair and pink cheeks" (the Misses Bliss were as brown as hot-cross buns). "But I've often felt like telling poor Mrs. Wotherspoon that her daughter was overdressed, especially when I saw her come out, just now, in white cloth lined with rose-color and bordered with chinchilla fur. So theatrical, I think, don't you?"

"I heard Brook himself say last summer at Newport that the girl looked like a fashion plate on rollers," remarked Josephine. "But perhaps she will get over that second-rate taste when she marries Brook. At any rate, Mrs. Brook can dress as she pleases."

At a Winter House-Party

"Should you think a white cloth skating costume would be becoming to Clara?" asked Mrs. Bliss, a little anxiously.

"Clara's brown and crimson is so perfect," answered Miss Brenton, loyally, while helping herself to another *paté* sandwich; and Mrs. Bliss allowed herself to be convinced.

As the door on the lake side of the house opened, at this moment, to let in, on a burst of frosty air as stirring as the blare of a trumpet, a group of merry chattering young people, — conspicuous among whom was the white-vestured maiden under recent discussion, — Gwendolyn Talcott, her fur collar pulled up well around her cheeks, a little black veil drawn down over her eyes, started to pass out along the way by which they came.

"Oh! I wanted so much to talk to

At a Winter House-Party

you about being Secretary to our new Society for Inducing Citizens not to Strew Paper in the Streets," interposed her hostess, with a sort of parenthetical breathlessness that was common to her.

"Another time," said Gwendolyn. She longed to be out of the atmosphere in which she was beginning to believe the best part of her had been wrecked. Passing through the incoming crowd, she found a boy to put on her skates, and was soon along with her thoughts, speeding swiftly over the farthest confines of the lake.

At eighteen, she had "come out," as lovely and blooming and impetuous a young creature as one would wish to see. Her father, well born, indulgent, and of ample means, had placed her in uncontrolled possession of the reins of his establishment. All of his friends, and a new crop of her own, had speedily arisen to do her homage.

Had she been of a less masterful disposition, no doubt Miss Talcott would have married early, and at the present moment would have been filling a place in the ranks of young matrons elate with hackneyed joys. But, at first, she was intoxicated by her opportunity for power. Her scope to rule, to adjust, to dictate other people's affairs had proved too tempting. Gwendolyn had verily believed that her fine intuitions were entrusted to her for the use of humanity at large. No sacrifice of self, no exertion, was too great so long as she could be informing her fellow-beings of what was best for them. By these efforts, she dreamed of moulding her own life into some new Titanic form, at which women condemned to mediocrity might gaze, on its pedestal in the chilly corridors of the temple of Fame.

To such an exalted frame of mind, suitors, naturally, were a jarring interruption. Those who presented themselves were refused by her with the gentle severity of one misunderstood. She told her father, once, with heavenly magnanimity, that she was not angry with a man who had asked her to be his wife, but disappointed, because she had thought him possessed of a higher intelligence than the

At a Winter House-Party

rest. This lover was Louis Brook, and three years later, he had repeated his offer, with the same success.

In the interval Gwendolyn's boundless energy of character and her splendid health, had sent her upon a steeple-chase after charity and philanthropy, that resulted, on the whole, in wasting a great deal of her time, and in confirming in wrong-doing many dependents upon society. She had many disappointments, and of disillusions not a few.

After that, Miss Talcott's intellect assumed sovereign control of her. Study, research, discussions of all questions of the day that could with convenience be taken up by one of her age and sex, and of some that had better have been left untouched, absorbed her waking hours. In crowded gatherings for social interchange, she pleased herself by fancying her own a lonely spirit, and, as a consequence, was often left alone in body. Every-day people soon tire of superiority, and forsake it as cheerfully as congregations do the clergyman after he has shut up his sermon case for another week.

Still, Miss Talcott was not without her vogue, and as a figure-head of originality was put forward by her friends whenever a demand for that variety of womankind was made. People looked to her to arise if there were a visiting author, or foreign *bel esprit*, before whom it was deemed necessary to illustrate American culture spelt with a capital C.

At a Winter House-Party

In the case of a gathering of exclusive fashion like the one now convened by Mrs. Algy Bliss, it was also natural to expect to see Miss Talcott present, even though hers was fast becoming in gay society a rather monumental pose.

The two people whom, during her years of experiment, Gwendolyn had most nearly admitted to her intimacy, were her father and Louis Brook. The first, because he was always cheerful, long-suffering, and brave enough to kiss her in the middle of one of her dissertations, and to go off down town. The second, since nothing that had passed between them had robbed her of his friendship, or of his evident preference for her society. For six long years, in season and out, Brook

At a Winter House-Party

had been in the habit of visiting her, walking with her, dropping in to dinner on Sunday evenings, writing her nice notes, and sending her new books and flowers. Except during the brief periods when he had lost his head and proposed, he had always preserved toward her the attitude of quiet receptivity of her ideal man. Two or three weeks before the present date, he had gone across the continent on a matter of business; and, until Mrs. Bliss had announced the fact, Gwendolyn did not even know of his return eastward. As to his sentimental alliance with the prettiest *débutante* of the year, she had not dreamed of the like of that! A sensation so much akin to an electric shock as the hint of it had not fallen to her experience — and yet she was not afraid!

She recollected, now, that the pretty child had made timid overtures to her since they had been first thrown together here yesterday. She had several times caught Gracie's eyes fixed upon her face with a reverential expression, to which, however, Gwendolyn was rather too accustomed from young admirers to have made especial note of it, in this case. But, flying, still, over the glassy plain, as the evening shadows gathered upon the valley, and in the opal of the sky shone a crescent moon, she felt a resentful rush of blood into her cheeks.

Brook's wife — this callow intelligence, this mere piece of prettiness! And her people his — worse and worse! It was inconceivable that he should allow himself to be dragged out of his element and landed upon that distinctly foreign shore. Brook, a calm, clear-sighted, refined, intellectual man, who could not, any more than herself, abide the veneered side of society; who had always shrunk from contact with the types of the Wotherspoon variety; who was noted for his exclusion of show people from his intimacy — as well expect him to put on cap-and-bells and dance a fandango in the middle of a cotillon. The story was, evidently, one of Josephine's ingenuities of annoyance. Who, as well as Gwendolyn, could know the absurdity of it; who as well understand that in reality Brook had been for years entirely content with the rôle she had apportioned to him?

At a Winter House-Party

From the incredulous mood, she passed into one of retrospect. For the first time in her life, perhaps, she thought more of Brook than of herself. Their experiences together, unrolled in memory, showed him wise, patient, forbearing with her, because his strength of character enabled him to be so. There had never, in her acquaintance, been a man so noble, so truly fit to share and guide an ambitious woman's life. If he had a fault, it was an indolence of manner that encouraged her own impetuosity; yet who would want to go through life with a man exactly like oneself! . . . Oh, no! There was nobody like Brook!

Tossing her head, Gwendolyn laughed aloud. In her absorption she had not noticed that the lake was now free of skaters. One of the two men who were about to rake out the bonfires came to her, speaking civilly.

"I beg pardon, miss; but there's been some mistake, I think. The boy, that was told to tell you when the last carriage was ready to start, ran home to his supper, and they've all gone and left you. If you'll step inside the tea-house, of course Mrs. Bliss

At a Winter House-Party

will be sending back for you presently. It wouldn't be more than half an hour to wait, at the longest."

"Oh! it's no matter, I'll walk," she answered, with more suavity than the countryman had expected from this handsome, haughty young lady.

"No doubt you'll meet the trap, miss," he said, while unbuckling her skates. "If you like, I'll go with you."

But Gwendolyn would not hear of this. She revelled in the prospect of a solitary tramp under the new moon and the sparkling planets that gemmed the steely sky. As she set off through the woods, her nostrils were greeted by faint delicious scents of forest spicery, and the dead leaves underfoot, powdered with rime, gave forth a sound as pleasant to her ear as the tinkle of the streamlet that, in spots, escaped from its glittering prison, and prattled of Spring to come.

It was cold, as the night drew on apace, but the air was dazzling clear. Was it rapid exercise, or a new joy bounding in her bosom, that exhilarated her so gloriously? Was the world really renewed

At a Winter House-Party

in beauty, or had she just been born again into it? Her cares, her doubts, her fears, had fallen away; she felt gay and lightsome, and ready for any frolic enterprise. Catching a silvery thread of swift-running water from a spring on the hill above, was a trough by the roadside; she bent over to taste of it, and could feel that her lips and her cheeks were glowing, but not with cold.

Through the dusk of the high-road, she presently sighted approaching her the bright tip of a cigar. Something told her that Brook was coming; and, for the first time in their intercourse, she felt her heart leap up within her at his approach. As he materialized from the shadows and greeted her in the old familiar quiet way, she did not even pretend to be surprised; it was all so much in answer to her thoughts.

"Of course, when I found out that you were left behind," he said, "I asked to be put out of the wagonette to walk back, on the probability that you would prefer setting out on foot to waiting. You see, I got to the tea-house just in time to return with the last party; and as soon as it was discovered you should have been with us, I quitted them. The carriage, however, will no doubt be soon upon us."

And, in effect, the carriage lamps were perceived, in a moment, gleaming on the descent of a steep bit of hill, ahead.

"How tiresome, when I had far rather walk!" she exclaimed, with almost the wilful intonation of a child.

She had let her hand rest in his, and Brook was struck by this unusual action, and by a joyous thrill in her voice. It, somehow, carried him back to the day of her *début*, when she had stood in a high white frock before a screen of the bouquets sent by her father's friends, and curtsied to half New York.

"There is really no good reason why we should take the carriage," he said, laughing. So the coachman (not surprised, for the retainers of Mrs. Bliss were warranted never to be taken aback by the vagaries of a house-party) was ordered to turn around and go back without them; and the horses started briskly homeward.

Thus the two pedestrians had to themselves the silent, starlit world, the fields about them guarded by couchant hills, here and there farm-house or cottage lights trembling out upon the slopes.

For a time Gwendolyn, her hands clasped in her muff, kept quietly in step with her companion, in the road bordered on either side by banks showing dim *chevaux de frise* of bare thorns and alder bushes and dead mullein spears. She did not want to spoil the hour by trite questions about trains and time tables and telegrams.

On Brook, also, the spell of reticence had descended.

"How beautiful this is!" he said, at length, in a voice that did not seem to her quite natural.

"And we are to have it for a whole day and evening yet, and part of another day still," she answered, almost exultingly.

"I always told you you should have lived in the country," he returned. "But then, what would have become of your mission to help your fellow-beings — though, I suppose, one fellow-being, if he were all you could get hold of, would be as big a jewel in your crown as a lot of them that came to you easily. Still, you could never have borne monotony."

"Oh! don't remind me of my mistakes," she cried. "That is the way you have often ended by condemning me seriously when you began to say something quite light and airy."

"I have never intentionally condemned you — or judged you, as to that. You have been the one person of my acquaintance privileged to confuse my sense of —"

"I hope you were not going to add, right and wrong?" she said, as he paused.

"Hardly that. But I think I might have saved you from some of the annoyances I let you run upon, simply because you went at them with such splendid dash — such belief in your own infallibility — a sort of an archangel's swoop through the ether, it seemed to me."

"What a vain bruised mortal it generally was that you ran to help after her fall, and set to preening her borrowed pinions! Ah, well! I have learned wisdom. Those days are over, forever. Hereafter, I am going to creep instead of swooping."

At a Winter House-Party

"This is not creeping, certainly. Your tread is so light and almost martial. It is delightful to me to think of you as vigorous and hopeful at a time in a young woman's experience when so many of them look pulled-down and disheartened and uncertain."

Surprised by his tone, she turned quickly toward him.

"This sounds like a valedictory. Or are you making late amends for previous hard judgment?"

"No; but I, who have borne with you the strain of the fray, feel privileged to congratulate you upon approaching victory. I believe you are going to be happier hereafter. Something tells me you are to find your long-sought clue to life; and, believe me, I — even I — can rejoice in it."

"Even you? Why, what do you mean? If it were not you, I should say there is a tinge of bitterness in your voice. That is what I don't look for from you who have spoiled me — perhaps!"

"Perhaps — though I don't know that I would recall it, if I could."

At a Winter House-Party

"At any rate, you have nothing with which to reproach yourself; and it is I who have suffered all," she said, with an attempt at lightness, half alarmed at the unwonted gravity of his manner.

"Suffered," he burst forth, as if irresistibly. "Great heavens! I believe you don't know the meaning of the word! Suppose you had been condemned to serve one purpose with all your might, for years, until long waiting for reward had rusted your heart's core. A hundred times, I have said to myself, 'She is a woman who has cultivated herself to catch every echo of human woe and solace it, and yet she plays with mine.' And now you say, 'It is I who have suffered all.'"

Gwendolyn, although greatly perturbed, did not answer. She was gathering up her forces for the belated avowal she had determined presently to yield him; the avowal so richly deserved, that would make their past a blank, and flood their future with delight. In the interval, it was almost a luxury to hear herself thus denounced by him.

"Yes; a hundred times," he went on,

At a Winter House-Party

"and oftener, I have left you, wounded to the quick. If there had been another Richmond in the field, I'd have dropped out long ago; but I knew, I knew, that I gave you the companionship no other man could offer, so I stifled my passion and resumed my patient attitude. Your dependence on me was my only requital. It was a poor part to play, I grant you; but for your sake I played it; and still you gave no sign. That you did feel my love and divine my hope, I could not for a moment insult your intuition by doubting. I even believe you liked to feel it, and to know that, when you chose, at the lifting of a finger, you could secure the pleasant emotion an expressive response to it would cause you."

"Oh! But that *is* cruel," she exclaimed, between quick breaths.

"Cruel, perhaps. If it is unjust, God forgive me, for I have suffered much. Consider, Gwendolyn, it is six years of a man's life you have appropriated, and given him nothing in return. There has not been a hairy dirty crank from any other country that brought a fad to our shores, whose lot you would not have set yourself to ameliorate in preference to mine. I shouldn't have felt this to be a wrong, mark you, had I not believed that, deep down in the bottom of that veiled heart of yours, there was all along an intention to put me, some day, out of my misery by making me your husband. But even that illusion went at last, and the result—"

He stopped. She was trembling so violently that he extended his arm to steady her; then abruptly withdrew it, and laid, instead, her hand within his arm. When Gwendolyn felt she could control her voice, her words came out with a passionate flow and emphasis that astonished beyond measure the man who had thought he knew her better than any one.

"I see it all, now. Oh! Go on; say more; say anything, if it is a relief to you. I suppose mine was one of those crimes the law doesn't reach; but God is my witness, I did not mean to go so far. I think a girl can't always understand what a man may feel for her, even if she —I was vain, presumptuous, overbearing, if you please, but I was innocent of real harm — Harm? — to *you* — "

Could that indeed be Gwendolyn, so arch, so sad, so proud, so humble, so tender, so enchanting? She would not heed his movement as if to hold her back.

"It is true, all true, what you said, just now. You saw right, you read my real self. Since I've known you, there was never really a moment — "

"In pity, Gwendolyn," he exclaimed, hoarsely interrupting her.

They had reached the crest of a hill and, over on the slope beyond, saw the great dark mass of the house facing them, light shining from every window. As she paused bewildered, he started away from her, making a gesture in its direction. Her arm, freed from his, dropped by her side, and they walked, mechanical, speechless, to the gateway of the lodge, where a hanging lamp revealed their faces to each other.

They exchanged one wretched glance; and in that moment something went out of his life, and out of hers, that was to come back no more.

The Secret of San Juan

The Secret of San Juan

Part I

A SCORE of years after our war between the States, Lloyd Sargent, of Boston, a young man whose passion for the remote and picturesque had led him to investigate in person many of the combinations of fable and reality presented by the old world, before settling down to the search for romantic color in his own country, was cruising in his little yacht, *Campaspe*, off the shores of southern Georgia. The boat, chartered from a western millionnaire who had built it for the pleasure of his family in southern waters, proved at the first hint of rough seas to be a mere exasperating toy that must needs fly for safe keeping into the nearest harbor; but dur-

The Secret of San Juan

ing the long stretches of brilliantly clear weather common to that region, when she would glide swiftly under a sky as blue as Italy's, in the shallows along shores fringed with silvery palmettos, her deck was a lotos-eater's paradise.

One evening, at sunset, following a favorite caprice, Sargent directed his native pilot to turn inward from the bay, through a narrow passage that cleft a wide verdurous plain of grass and reeds and flowers. Soon the *Campaspe* was apparently ashore. All before, behind, around her, was a mass of waving, glistening green arched by the pearly radiance of the sky. So fantastically winding was the inlet along which she nosed her way, she seemed at moments to be running headlong into a morass, out of an island of aquatic vegetation. Far eastward, Sargent espied the sails of ships, like white birds winging their way over the marsh; and his ear was not forsaken by the swash of the surf upon the outer beach. But, practically, he had Nature for his own.

After a while, standing to survey the

scene beside the man at the wheel, he caught, away over the green boundaries of creation, a red lustre that could be nothing but the level rays of the sun striking a window pane.

"A house, with trees?" he said, in surprise. "I don't remember to have seen one at that point."

"Because we've never come in this way before, sir," answered the pilot. "It's built on a little neck o' land runnin' out of a bit of jungle over yonder. Queer people live there, Mr. Sargent. I've often thought of asking if you wouldn't like to take a look at 'em."

"Who are your queer people, Adams?" asked the young man, who had before encouraged his guide's loquacity in local chronicles. "And, while you are telling me, by all means let's run over and have a look at them. If they have fresh eggs and milk to sell, so much the better for our commissariat."

"Aye, sir, and honey too, if you're fond o' that article. Peter Parsons, the head o' the family, is a famous bee hunter in these parts. He's an old man now, and has got three sons and three daughters well on in life, that's livin' there with him. None of them got married, cos none o' that stock ever married out o' their own connection, and their supply o' wives and husbands has 'bout run short, I reckon. Curious matter that, sir. Sence time out o' mind, them folks have been livin' there; and they all came out o' two families that was brought over from England, they say, by old Governor Oglethorpe with the people he imported to colonize the State o' Georgy with; settled here in the swamp, and intermarried, till now they've dwindled down to three old cracker maids and three old cracker bachelors, all o' the same parents. Last year the old woman died, and they put her away in the family burying-ground somewheres in the swamp, nobody knows where. Fact is, it's all guess-work about the Parsonses concerns, anyway. Nobody I ever knowed has crost their door-sill; and only onst in a long time people get a sight of the old man in his boat. They grow corn, and beat it between two stones for their meal; and cotton, that they spin and weave into cloth to make their clothes out er. None of 'em can't read or write; and they do say the Parsonses never heard tell o' the war the time it lasted; an', seein' as I've got a bullet from the fight at Ellerson's Mill, in Virginny, rollin' around in me somewheres at this ere blessed minute, and old Parsons is as hale and sound as ever he was, I can't help wishing I'd been situated so as I didn't hear of it, nuther."

Sargent, beguiled by the man's prattle, did not realize the distance they had traversed in following the doublings of their watery way, till the *Campaspe*, saucy and triumphant, slid out of the marsh into the lakelet surrounding the cracker settlement. The banks of the little peninsula upon which a few decaying cabins built of logs were huddled together, beneath gaunt pines, were so gnawed by the action of the tides as to leave the roots of the trees hanging bare over them. But there was space reclaimed from the marsh at one side for a garden, together with a plot or two of grain; and from the window of a shanty, propped by piles over the

The Secret of San Juan

flood, a meek-faced old horse looked out with wonder at the newcomers. Behind all, stretched the inky shadows of a wall of jungle. From the chimney of one of the huts a faint waft of smoke signified inhabitance. But of sound there was none, except the flop of mud-turtles into the coffee-colored waters, the far cry of a loon, and the note of night-birds already beginning their communings in the deep tangle of the woods.

"Impossible to imagine a gloomier spot for human habitation," said Sargent, quite under the spell of the scene, and the skipper's tale of these melancholy folk.

"It ain't, so to speak, cheerful, sir," was the answer. "Might's well be a dead house, for all the notice they take of us. Seein' you're interested in these parts, Mr. Sargent, supposin' we take a short cut through the woods, and come out by San Juan Island, where you can see a real old style quality mansion. Could tell you stories about that house, sir, would make your flesh creep."

"Agreed," said Sargent, smiling. "Just as soon as we see whether we can make an impression upon this cracker fortress, and coax from them some of their merchandise, I'm with you."

All in vain the pretty *Campaspe* blew her whistle before the unresponsive huts. No face appeared at a window, no form at a door; and, at last, disgusted with the incivility of the boors within, Sargent gave orders to pursue their course.

They now turned sharp into a little creek threading their ever sinuous way through a cypress wood dense with growths, gnarled, misshapen, serpent-like. The trees, springing from mossy hummocks, were wrapped and strangled in vines and pendent moss. In the accumulation of dead leaves and black ooze on either side of the stream, the deadly moccasin, with frogs, turtles, and other subaqueous small fry, kept up a repulsive animation. From the elevation of the yacht's bridge, Sargent, well satisfied to maintain this distance from their base of operations, descried through an opening between the trees, at still a considerable way ahead, an object that he took to be a boat. Then a twist in the channel caused him to lose sight of

The Secret of San Juan

it before he could be certain it was not a floating log.

"It would be a brave voyager who would venture in here alone, at this hour," he said to Adams.

"If it's anybody, it's old man Parsons himself, I reckon," was the reply. "But there ain't many likely to be round here. The nighest family lives at San Juan, where we are goin' to."

"You were about to tell me more of them," said Sargent, good-naturedly.

"It's a grand family, the Trevelyans, sir, regular tip-toppers; but they've pretty much run out now. The island's belonged to them since the State was settled, and 'cept for the four years when the master was away fighting for the Confederacy, there's some on 'em always lived there. But it's been an unlucky house, sir. Accidents, and duels, and sudden deaths, and misfortins o' one kind or another, always happenin' in every generation. Before the war broke out, Capt'n Trevelyan's—that's the present owner, sir—father an' mother died within a day o' each other, and the Capt'n went off up the country an' married his first cousin, like the Trevelyans always did. She was the child o' first cousins, and so was he; so the Trevelyan blood now is pretty much of a muchness, and the Capt'n and his wife and daughter are as like each other as peas in a pod. Well, sir, the Capt'n's young wife stayed with her parents in the northern part of the State, while he went to the war, and for four years the island grew wild, without nobody to look after it but a few niggers in their cabins that 'lected to keep on stayin' there. Then the Capt'n was badly wounded in one of the battles around Richmond, and laid for months in the hospital there, 'fore they patched him up so as he could get home to his wife. Nuthin' would do him but to come back to live on San Juan. But what with fire, and armies, and relations dyin' off, and losing property, the Trevelyan family ain't what they used to be. There ain't much prospect for their child—the girl that was born at San Juan soon after the war."

"Then there is no son?"

"There was one, sir," said the man,

dropping his voice. "The young lady is the livin' image of the Capt'n, when I first see him in the war. The gayest, open-handedest, handsomest, young officer in his brigade. They say his heart's bound up in Miss Ariana."

"Ariana, by George!" exclaimed Sargent; "there's a name for you."

"It's a family name, sir," answered the man, who saw nothing to smile at. "I've only seen the young lady once, myself, when I took a sailing party in near their shore to get a look at the island; and then she was riding her tackey poney into the surf to give it a bath. A regular beauty, Mr. Sargent — a dare-devil Trevelyan all over; pity there ain't any better look-out for her, or anybody good enough to marry her, and take her away from the wreck o' that old tumble-down house and family."

"You are not consistent in your sympathy for the Captain," observed the young man, upon whom this bold charge had been made with a sidewise glance, half-cunning, half-pathetic.

"Oh, sir! but I haven't told you.

When you know all that's happened at San Juan since the war, and all that's feared may happen there, you'll understand me better."

"Then go on with your yarn; though I can't say it's inspiriting in such surroundings."

"Well, sir, the story about their only son is well known hereabouts. He was a beautiful boy, six years old, and full o' spirits; and one evening, in the dark, he went outside to play he was a wild cat. Bein' a good climber, he got out on a branch of a tree near the house where the leaves nearly covered him, and made a sound to imitate the creeter he was pretendin' fur to be. The Capt'n, hurrying to the door with his gun, fired in the direction of the noise — and — deed, sir, I'm the father of a little kid myself, an' it chokes me to this day — down fell the youngster, dead!"

"Good heavens!" exclaimed the listener.

"Yes, sir, dead — and he lies in the buryin' ground of the island, one of a little row of graves with black crosses over 'em. For, after that, the Capt'n's wife's heart broke; more babies were born, but her children never throve. The only one of the lot that survived to grow up strong and hearty was Miss Ariana. I kinder wish you could make acquaintance with the young lady, Mr. Sargent. She's prettier than any of them that come down here pleasurin' in winter time — and I've steered many a party of fine folks through these waters. It's foolish, maybe, but we people round here respects the old Trevelyan name; and, now it's about goin' under, we'd like to see one of the breed saved from the fate of the rest of 'em."

"You are a creature of infinite conceit, Adams," said his employer, amused. "But what else is it you hint at about the present condition of the family at San Juan?"

"Nobody knows, sir. It's all rumor, but there's an idee goin' the rounds that the mistress is insane, and may do damage to her husband and daughter. She's not shut up, that's certain; for ole Fishin' Dick, who lives on the island, told me she buys fish from him at the door, quite regular; but she's dead white lookin', he says, and her black eyes glitter; and she ain't never seen to smile since her boy was shot."

"And no wonder. But 'the Capt'n'—has he, poor man, ever held up his head since the tragedy?"

"That's the strange part of it, sir. Fishin' Dick says he's about with the young lady sailin' and ridin' and gunnin', quite lively and cheerful; looks like a boy himself, and seems not to mind anything so long as he's got his daughter's company. Only the madam never leaves the house—"

"Look out!" suddenly shouted Sargent in a voice of thunder.

They had been rounding the last bend of a bow-knot in the stream. In the shadows directly ahead of them, he saw a canoe paddled by a solitary figure clothed in white; and heard from it a cry of warning in a woman's voice.

Before the engines could be reversed the canoe had sheered off to one side; but, in escaping collision with the yacht, it ran upon the sharp end of a sunken branch, and capsized immediately.

Sargent, on the lower deck in a moment, was not so quick as a young sailor in his employ, who throwing a rope to the struggling woman, contrived with dexterity to bring her alongside the yacht's steps, by which simple means she was helped aboard, before she had fairly realized her plight.

But it was Sargent whose hand met hers, to whom she addressed herself in a voice singularly soft.

"It was my fault, not yours," she said; "when I heard you coming, I stopped to wonder who it could be, instead of getting out of the way. It isn't often any kind of a steamboat comes along our creek, you know."

"I can only be thankful that you are safe," he exclaimed, fervently. "I was never so horrified as when I saw you go into that loathsome water."

"You are more afraid of snakes and turtles than I am, who have been brought up among them," she answered, shaking out a mass of night-dark hair with a movement all womanly, and striving to wring the water from the skirt of a shabby cotton gown.

Sargent, who beheld in his treasure-trove one of the most beautiful young women he had ever seen, divined at once that he had secured as a passenger the daughter of San Juan.

"I am sorry that we have no ladies aboard," he said, with courtesy; "but my cabin is at your disposal, and so is the yacht, for that matter. You will find in there a mackintosh, at least, and if you will direct us where to take you —"

"I am Miss Trevelyan of San Juan," she said, with a touch of hauteur; "and my father's house is not very far from here. Might I trouble you to have my canoe brought aboard, and see if it is fit for me to get into again?"

"Not until you have had some wine or something," he persisted; "and I'm afraid I must insist upon that mackintosh."

"And I insist upon getting into my canoe," she said, with childish wilfulness.

But the canoe, upon recovery, proving to have received from the bough a disabling wound, Miss Trevelyan was compelled to withdraw from her attitude of superiority.

"Please take me home," she said, tears

starting suddenly to her eyes. "It's too dreadful to think of papa, if you hadn't picked me up. He doesn't like me to come in here after the sun goes down; but I'm not a bit afraid, and I did so want to get some of the Parsons' guinea eggs for his supper. And now they are gone, poor things—Oh! no, there's my egg-basket floating. Do, please, somebody, bring it in with a boathook."

"Certainly, if you will put on this," replied Sargent, after disappearing for a moment to return with the rejected mackintosh, the steward attending him with a glass of sherry on a tray. "And drink this," he added, smiling, though with a note of authority in his voice.

"Yes, yes, only save my egg-basket," she said, appealingly; and, his behests accomplished, Miss Trevelyan had the satisfaction of seeing the contents of the canoe brought safely aboard, including a large gourd covered with a white cotton cloth in the basket with the eggs, which she hailed with heart-felt satisfaction.

"So that is what became of the good things I didn't get?" exclaimed Sargent.

"They are so cross to strangers, those poor Parsons," she answered, apologetically; "when they've nothing to sell, they won't come to the door, even. But few people go there, and if it were not for old Peter with his boat, they wouldn't sell much of anything. I'll give you some of my honey, if you like. It's the best you ever tasted; out of the heart of the swamp old Peter gets it, and it smells of magnolia blossoms — see!"

Sargent did not know whether to make her his guest, or leave her to herself. To the delight of old Adams, who received her like a princess, the young lady insisted upon mounting to the bridge, where, her tears, if not her garments, already dried, she enjoyed, as if it had been a pleasure mapped out for her, the novel experience of her homeward voyage.

And now the sailors came up and lighted behind them knots of pitch-pine heaped in an open brazier set on the upper deck, that flared with magnificent effect into the vault of branches meeting overhead and woven together with vines and parasites. By this illumination all the

The Secret of San Juan

higher mysteries of the forest were suddenly laid bare; even the birds in their nests, like black patches against the sky, were seen through the tracery of leaves. It was a wonder-world of tropic luxuriance, at which Ariana clapped her hands with joy.

"Oh! never, never," she exclaimed, "have I seen our woods like this. I shall tell papa what a delight you have given me; and he will thank you better than I can."

Was she child or woman? Sargent could not tell. He only knew that her presence exhaled a charm inexpressible, that her face was beautiful as a dream of a southern night.

Part II

AS gay *Campaspe*, leaving the noisome gloom of the swamp, sped through another green and fertile plain to seek the open water of the coast, behold! San Juan lay before her, as if blocking her progress to the eastward, along the shore.

Viewed in the clear of evening, a silver surf curling upon its belt of sand marble-white, its surface overgrown with woodland that shook out spicy odors upon the breeze — the white walls of its old stuccoed mansion gleaming through orange and myrtle, bay and roses — Miss Trevelyan's home justified to the full local pride in its beauty. But to Sargent's praises of the island the girl hardly lent ear, so intent was she in gazing at a point of the shore, on the bay side, where a landing came into view.

"I see him now! He's there, with old Joshua, wondering with all his might at your pretty little steam-yacht. How surprised he'll be to know that I am aboard of her," she exclaimed, joyously; then, arching both hands over her mouth, she gave vent to a long cry, clear as a bird's note, to which there was speedy answer from the landing.

When the yacht ran close to the wharf, Sargent saw coming to meet them across the rotting boards a handsome man, so youthful in appearance as to make it hard to believe he was not Ariana's brother rather than her father, and with a bright, trustful look in his eyes that was Ariana's own. Dressed in a suit of home-spun cotton, and wearing a broad-brimmed hat plaited of palmetto straw, there was no other token of the rustic about Guy Trevelyan's appearance; and his manner in receiving his daughter's explanations, as well as her new acquaintance, was full of her easy grace. Adams was right. These two scions of an ancient, hapless house were strikingly alike in person; and from the glad manner of their meeting, Sargent correctly judged that their lives were entwined in love for each other.

"It is really the first time this wild

rover of mine has ever come to serious grief," said Trevelyan. "And now, Mr. Sargent, you will let me show my appreciation of your care of her, by spending at least the night with us. Oh! we will take no denial, if you can put up with plain fare and lodging. People call it an interesting old house; and you will find no better anchorage for the yacht than in our little bay, here. It will be a variety upon your cruise; and we'll give you, if nothing more, a southern welcome."

There was no gainsaying hospitality like this; and in a short time Sargent was strolling, between his host and the young lady, under an avenue of live oak and olive canopied with the luscious blooms of yellow jasmine, and so planned to divide the island that, at the far end of the road, they caught a glimpse of the bounding surf on the outer beach beyond.

Sargent, until they were well on their way in this bowery path, did not observe that their footsteps were accompanied by a man of middle age, meanly dressed, with a pallid complexion and deep-set, sombre eyes, stooping at the shoulders, but yet of a build suggesting great physical strength, who had taken his bag from a sailor, and was carrying it after them.

Trevelyan, seeing his guest glance inquiringly at this attendant, did not think it necessary to comment upon the circumstance; but Ariana said, in her soft voice, "He is a deaf mute, poor fellow; one of the sons of old Peter Parsons, whose house you passed in the marsh. He has lived with us — oh, ever so long; and my mother nursed him through a serious illness. He follows my father like a dog. I don't think Joshua could have a contented minute, if papa were out of his sight."

"A grewsome comrade in perpetuity," Sargent thought, while rather surprised at the fact that Mr. Trevelyan appeared not to hear his daughter's explanation. But as at this juncture they emerged from the cloying sweetness of the jasmine grove into an open plateau in the centre of the island, his attention was claimed by the old mansion of San Juan.

Ancient and mouldering, the chimneys leaning out of line, the roof bulging in places and sunk in others, the balustrade of the plaisance on top fallen away under the weight of roses, the windows in chief part hermetically sealed, the walls of tabby plaster stained by the tempests of a century — Nature had yet so enwrapped and embalmed the old house in leaves and flowers, it seemed to be springing from a huge bouquet.

"'A poor thing, but mine own,' Mr. Sargent," said his host, pausing to cast an affectionate glance upon his dwelling, before conducting his guest inside of it.

Upon the flag-stone of the front door, Sargent started at the apparition of a large black snake writhing across his pathway. Seeing the visitor's look of irrepressible disgust, the mute dashed nimbly forward, and, with two blows of a stout stick he carried, disposed of the offending reptile. Sargent was quite unprepared for the pallor that swept across his host's face at this incident, and the dilation in his eyes as if of fear.

"You must get over your antipathy to snakes, if you want to enjoy our island, Mr. Sargent," laughed Ariana in the young man's ear. "It isn't uncommon for the negroes at work here to find them curling about their legs; and if only they do not *rattle*, we do not mind. But you know papa can't bear to have anything killed near the house."

Sargent was amazed that she should so lightly hazard such an allusion to a tragedy that must be still bleeding in her father's memory. But Trevelyan, now quite himself again, had preceded them into the house and, turning upon the threshold with quaint, old-fashioned courtesy, was in the act of bidding his guest welcome to San Juan.

It was quite dark as they entered, until a negro girl, barefoot and stealthy, came from behind a door, holding in her hand a candle of bog-myrtle wax in a heavy silver candlestick, by the faint light of which Sargent saw that they were in the panelled hall with wide double staircase, familiar to frequenters of southern houses.

Ariana having melted, as it seemed, into the panelling, her father, announcing that supper was almost ready, led the way before Sargent into a room in a wing on the ground floor, where a four-posted bed, an armchair, a washing-stand, and a dim mirror over a mahogany chest of drawers, supplied the necessaries for his toilet.

Left alone in his chamber, Sargent abandoned himself to musing over the strange impressions he had received. Trevelyan's beauty, distinction; his mercurial temper; the dreadful story that had apparently left so little imprint upon him; the depressing comradeship of his mute shadow; the incident of the killing of the snake; and above all, Ariana's charming contradictions of manner and character — excited their guest's keenest speculation. An odd feature of the situation was that, during his entire conversation with the young girl and her father, neither of them had mentioned the lady of the house, except when Ariana had touched lightly upon her mother's former work of mercy in nursing Joshua.

Of course it was as Adams had hinted. Mrs. Trevelyan, mentally unhinged by her sorrows, was by common consent of her family kept in the background of their speech. That he should see her, Sargent was glad not to believe; the consciousness of being under the same roof with her, was enough to make him wish that, save for the bright eyes of Ariana, he were again safely afloat in his yacht. Then, smiling at his feebleness of spirit, he answered a summons to supper.

The meal, served in a large, bare but stately apartment, was a new surprise to him. The table, set with rare antique damask and porcelain and silver, presented such dainties as roast marsh-hen, turtle in a silver dish that might have been offered to the palate of a king, a crab salad, with oranges and olives plucked from their own plantations, and Ariana's honeycomb to supplement the inevitable waffles. Coffee more savory than that dispensed by Miss Trevelyan from a Colonial urn surmounted by a large pineapple in beaten silver, Sargent could not remember to have tasted in Paris, or in the East; and at the close of the feast Trevelyan produced for him a dusty bottle of Madeira that had for long years been ripening under the sunshine that bathed the roof of the old house.

"Delicious," said the guest, as he tasted

the first sip of the fragrant nectar. "How is it that this has a flavor all its own?"

"That is our mystery," answered Trevelyan, beaming like a pleased boy. "It is almost the last of a lot laid down by my father forty years ago. But this much I can tell you: with us, good Madeira is not entombed in the gloom of a cellar underground; it is rather offered high up on the altar of the sun — in the garret."

During the progress of the meal, of which Trevelyan ate but sparingly — a couple of the little brown guinea eggs, fetched by Ariana from the house in the swamp, forming, indeed, the chief part of his repast — Sargent did not see the mute. The service of the table was performed by a purblind negro butler, wearing trousers of Confederate gray cloth, with an old dress-coat and a ruffled shirt, evidently assumed in honor of the occasion. But as Trevelyan, warmed with a glass or two of wine, waxed gay and even jovial, Sargent became conscious, by the movement behind a tall Chinese screen of black and gold set before the pantry-door, that their party was probably under observation by unseen eyes.

"It is that tiresome Shadow," he said to himself; "truly, there is a point at which loyal devotion can become abhorrent. But as long as my host and his beautiful daughter make no account of this unpleasant presence, it is surely not my affair to do so."

Ariana, vanishing for a time after the meal, rejoined them on the veranda, whither the two gentlemen had repaired to smoke their cigars under the light of a moon that now flooded earth and sea with radiance. So innocent her manner to him, that heretofore the young man had hardly felt more for her than an impulse of protecting admiration for a lovely and confiding child. But when Trevelyan, excusing himself, went into the house, Sargent recognized with a throb of vivid emotion that he was in danger of succumbing to a power no child ever wielded over man. Perhaps it was the inevitable march of fate; but at this hour, under this light, she looked like the embodiment of all he had ever pictured as most winning in a woman. Sitting, not upon the bench beside him, but opposite on the railing of the veranda under an arch of Cherokee roses, of which the flowers, in the argent gleam of the moon, looked as if sculptured from Parian marble, her shapely form and fair face were to him a revelation of delight. A passionate admiration and sympathy arose within him for this scion of an ill-starred race. He longed to snatch her from behind the veil of sadness and mystery that baffled him, and go with her out into the light of every day.

They talked long and of many things, Ariana revealing to him more and more the sweet lack of sophistication in her nature. He was, by now, quite convinced they had kept from her the true character of the tragedy of her brother's death, occurring when she was of tender years. But he had not fathomed other things concerning the relations of the household to each other; and, most of all, he was perplexed by the light-hearted insouciance of the host who, returning after a while to join them with all the gayety of a child, made the rest of the evening pass away merrily.

Sargent, again in his chamber, had no

desire to go to bed. But for a glimpse at the end of a leafy vista of his fairy yacht riding at anchor upon the illuminated bay, he would have thought himself under the delusion of a dream. Approaching one of the French windows that opened directly upon a little court embowered in lemon and orange trees, in the centre of which a tiny stream of water trickled into a ruined fountain surrounded by japonicas and cape-jasmines, he gazed for so long upon the bewitching pageant of the night, that at last he could not resist stepping out-of-doors to enjoy it further under the vault of heaven.

Hardly had he gained the seclusion of a clump of oleanders arching over what had once been a gravel-walk, than he heard a door open near him, and saw the noiseless appearance upon the step outside of it of a woman dressed in white, who, after a brief hesitation, glided out into the fuller light of the court, and turned her face in scrutiny of the windows of his own room.

Sargent saw at once that it was Ariana, and his heart leaped up at sight of her solitary beauty. Then he perceived upon her countenance a look foreign to Ariana's face, and, bewildered, he stood spellbound, wondering at the change. Surely mortal woman's eyes never expressed more of poignant sorrow, of abiding apprehension, than did this poor creature's, wandering alone into the night. As he stood debating whether to show himself and offer the help or counsel she seemed to need, another figure issued from the house, in whom Sargent recognized the mute.

This uncouth fellow, going swiftly to join the lady, was received by her with a manner of chiding, which he took with the patience of a loving dog. After they had talked for some little time together in a sign language Sargent could not understand, the man, while seeming to urge his point, took out of his pocket, and held up before her with chuckling and pathetic glee, a large iron key. At this, the lady appeared to give over her seeming opposition, and together they passed down the garden walk, and were swallowed in an abyss of shrubbery. Sargent did not stop to discuss with himself the ethics of the case, but, under the goad of a young man's infatuation, followed the pair.

The path along which they preceded him opened into an alley of dwarf trees, whose foliage had been long overgrown and smothered by masses of hanging moss that dropped like gray stalactites overhead, creating a gloom neither moon nor sun had power to penetrate. From this inexpressibly dreary passage, the couple ahead of Sargent diverged to an enclosure cleared out of the environing darkness of the wood, and walled with the tabby material peculiar to that vicinity. Here the broad moonlight held again full sway, and Sargent surmised that the spot was the burial-place of the Trevelyans. As if to typify the family's decadence in place and fortune, the tombs in the middle of the plot were large, costly, embellished with armorial bearings and pompous epitaphs; elsewhere arose simple headstones, and in a far corner, under the shelter of the broken wall, stood a row of five wooden crosses, marking little graves.

Swiftly approaching the largest of these tiny mounds, the lady upon whom Sargent's gaze was riveted dropped upon her knees; and then, bending over it with a burst of such impassioned grief as but one earthly love bestows upon the long-gone dead, she clasped with both arms the dust heaped over her buried hopes.

In a flash was revealed to the looker-on that this hapless mourner was not the daughter of the house, but the crazed mother, of whose singular resemblance to her child he now remembered Adams had spoken to him. With a thrill of shame at his intrusion, Sargent withdrew into the dense shade of the funereal avenue, but not before he had seen the mute, casting his own unwieldy bulk upon the ground beside his mistress, seem to plead with her in what could be nothing else than a rude attempt at consolation.

Retracing his steps, Sargent stood once more by the trickle of the fountain in the little court. What he had just seen touched him with deeper compassion, with tenderer sentiment, for Ariana. Reckless of consequence, he began turning over in his mind every conceivable plan by which it might be possible for him to come to her relief, assuage the distresses of her family, awaken in her a new sense of the joy of living — carry out, in effect, all the glorious, quixotic schemes ever engendered by fancy and moonshine, the plash of fountains, and the scent of flowers at midnight, in a young man's ardent brain.

At last, entering his chamber by way of the window as he had escaped, Sargent lingered, irresolute as to whether, under such environment, it were worth while to attempt to court sleep at all. Suddenly, the silence of the night was riven by a cry from within the house — a cry that sickened his heart, and robbed him for an instant of all strength — for it was one of mortal terror, and the voice was Ariana's.

Part III

SARGENT dashed to his bedroom door to find it locked on the outside. Outraged and reckless, he tried to force it, and failed; then, the awful cries continuing, bethought him of the door opening into the garden by which Mrs. Trevelyan had come out; and, springing through his window into the court, he ran toward it. As he had hoped, this barrier yielded at a touch, and he found himself at the foot of a flight of narrow stairs, steep and unlighted, up which he groped, his heart thumping his ribs at the ominous silence that had succeeded the horror of Ariana's shrieks.

Alas! at the top of the steps another locked door interposed itself between him and the poor girl he longed to succor. Again and again, with frenzied strength he threw himself against it in vain; again he heard Ariana's appeal for help, this time it seemed to him in weaker tones. Then, between impotence and uncertainty, he clenched his fists and swore at fate, drawing back to gather all his power for a final onslaught upon the door.

Simultaneously, there was a scramble up the stairs behind him; a figure flying like the wind brushed against him; pinning him against the wall, and uttering moans of anguish,—Sargent knew he should never forget to his dying day,—she put a key into the lock. After her bounded the mute, emitting sounds of unearthly anger, his great frame shaken with stertorous emotion. Hurling Sargent out of his path, the furious creature followed his mistress through the door, which immediately closed after them as with a spring.

Chafing and humiliated at his failure to be of use, horror in his heart at the possibilities of Ariana's fate, Sargent lingered, with an ear against the door, straining his sense of hearing, but not a sound again broke the dreadful silence of the house.

What had it been? After all, whatever Ariana's terror or extremity, had not her father been near to succor her? Sargent knew that, according to southern custom, the negro servants had gone away to sleep in their distant cabins; and, with the idea of detecting or intercepting some marauder, he walked around the house, looking up at the windows, and keeping an ear upon the shrubbery. In two of the upper bedrooms lights burned; he heard the murmur of low voices, but all signs of violent alarm had ceased. Could it have been a nightmare? In any case, Trevelyan, as his host, would assuredly soon come down to relieve the anxiety of his guest necessarily aroused by the disturbance. Had not Sargent seen the one person of the family from whom an unnatural outbreak might have been most counted upon, away from the house, he would certainly have charged Mrs. Trevelyan with Ariana's terrible experience. But not only the poor lady's absence, but her mien and actions exonerated her from such suspicion. If Sargent were a judge, she was no lunatic, but a loving, sorrow-smitten woman, crushed to earth by affliction, and shunning the eye of man. And what was that moan heard by him as she had rushed past him in the darkness of the stairway, if not an expression of agonizing fear for the safety of one dear as her own life?

These thoughts chased each other through Sargent's head till it felt like bursting. He went back to his room and waited there, seated by the door which, to his amazement, he had found locked. An hour, two hours passed, and Trevelyan did not appear. Finally, exhausted, the young man threw himself as he was upon the bed, and sleep gave him merciful relief.

From a deep slumber Sargent awoke next morning with a start. Through his windows the sunlight poured in a dazzling stream around him. In an orange-tree outside a mocking-bird sang with irresistible sweetness. From where he lay he could look out upon the blue sea-line laughing in matin brightness. All nature was awake, refreshed, exuberant. Only he carried in his bosom a heart like a stone.

For, in a second, it all came back to him. Stiff and sore he arose and went over to drink some water from a carafe left upon his table the night before. There, beside the tray with the water and glasses, lay a folded piece of paper. Quickly he went to the door and tried it; it had been unlocked and his visitor had come to him unperceived.

Sargent lost no time in speculation. Tearing open with a fevered hand the quaintly folded note, he looked first at the signature; to his joy it was Ariana's name.

"I am safe," was written in trembling characters, "but in great distress of mind. After what has passed, there is nothing for me but to ask you to go away from our most unhappy house. If you could come to the marsh-house Saturday, in the afternoon, I will try to be there and explain to you what it is due to you to know."

The man who devoured this poor little scrawl paused for a moment in uncertainty, then, hastily packing his bag, went out of the house wondering at the fervor of his desire to remain there.

Looking back, before the foliage should shut the old mansion from his sight, he paused, and, with a faint hope she might see him, raised his hat. But answer or token from her there was none. What might have been a wave of his lady's handkerchief from window or balcony was only the drift of white rose petals to the earth. With a deep sigh he strode on his way through the woods.

Vanished now was their charm for him. The million dew-drops, strung upon jasmine wreath and mossy stalactite, shone for him in vain. The rich odor of blossoms that courted his nostrils seemed to him akin to the fragrance of flowers on a coffin lid.

Adams, who greeted the master upon his return to the yacht, was of the private opinion that Mr. Sargent was about to go under with an attack of malarial fever. Nothing else could account to him for the prompt check upon his garrulous curiosity concerning the visit to San Juan.

Sargent, as long as the island remained in sight, and after it had passed into a pencilled streak upon the horizon, stood on deck, gazing in its direction. When well out again upon the dancing sea, he went below to his cabin, and remained there until they had made a landing.

A few days later, the yacht received orders from the hotel of the little town on the coast that was Sargent's headquarters for the nonce, to be again in readiness for a short cruise. Adams, when his employer came aboard, was as glad to welcome him in apparently good health, as he was to unburden himself of important gossip.

"You'll excuse the liberty, sir; but I'm mighty relieved to see you about again, lookin' like yourself. I made sure that day in the swamps had laid you up with chills and fevers. We people down here don't 'low it could hurt us, if we stayed there week in, week out. But folks from the Nawth is different, I've noticed. Mr. Sargent, sir, I saw Fishin' Dick from San Juan in town with a fine lot o' sea bass, yesterday, and there's bin a misfortin happened in the family. They've lost Josh. Parsons, sir, you may remember of seein', that deef and dumb feller that kept around always with the Capt'n."

"Lost him?" repeated Sargent.

"Yes, sir. Heart disease, they called it, that took him quite suddent; must ha' been the very day we left there. Fishin' Dick says the Parsonses came arter the body with a barge covered all over the deck with a load of fresh grass, and took him away lyin' flat atop of it, the old man a-polin', an' the rest uv 'em singin' hymns; and o' course nobody ain't any idee where he's buried. Considerable loss, Josh. was to the Trevelyan family, I reckon, though Dick hadn't seen any of 'em to hear how they was a-takin' it. Mr. Sargent, have you spoke to the doctor, sir? You look palish still, and kinder sickly; and there's stuff that'll knock spots out o' fever an' agur, if you only take it in time."

"Thank you, I shall do very well," said the young man, walking away.

Adams' tidings were a fresh opening of the wound he had tried hard to heal. And the fate of the poor, faithful mute excited in him anew the dark suspicions with which he had left San Juan. Was it indeed heart disease, or was the real cause of the unfortunate man's death hidden forever among the accursed mysteries that had made a victim of the sweetest, loveliest young girl Sargent had ever met? Bah! the mere thought of it was insufferable!

If Ariana fulfilled her promise of meeting him to-day, he should soon know better how to deal with the problem of her misfortunes. A thousand wild fancies had suggested themselves, of relieving her, each of them breaking in turn against the wall of difficulty that confronted it.

Leaving the *Campaspe* at some distance from the marsh-house, Sargent got into a canoe, and despite the warnings of Adams, that he had better let the wooded part of the swamp alone, paddled up the silver way leading to his destination.

When he came within sight of the Parsons' settlement, his heart misgave him lest Ariana had failed to come; but there, tethered to the rude wharf, was her well-remembered craft, patched, evidently by the negroes, to serve its former purpose of utility. The door of the one inhabited cabin being closed, Sargent could only paddle to and fro, awaiting events. Erelong, he was rewarded by Ariana's appearance upon the threshold.

It was clear daylight in which he now

beheld her, and he was at once conscious of a great change in her young face. But she came down to meet him with a flash of welcome in her eyes, and, asking him to secure his canoe at the wharf, led the way back to the house.

The room they entered was empty, save for a gaunt, impassive woman who, dressed in a homespun frock of archaic cut, sat spinning by a hearth where smouldered a few embers covered under for the afternoon. The clay floor, the few chairs and tables, testified to the most elementary notions of comfort on the part of their owners; but the place was clean, and Ariana, offering her friend a splint-bottomed chair, took one near him, and sat looking into his eyes with a plaintive deprecation that touched him to the core.

"You need not mind her," began the girl, indicating their companion. "Mary is poor old Joshua's twin, and like him is deaf and dumb. There is so much for me to say to you, and it is so hard to say it, I hardly know where to begin. But first, I must ask you to pardon us for the cruel way you were treated under our roof.

It is not like that that the Trevelyans have been accustomed to entertain their friends,—but it was kind and merciful of you to go—from my window I watched the *Campaspe* steam away—I could hardly believe that I had been on her deck,—it was as hard to realize that, only the day before, I had been a happy, wilful child, for whom life was one long, bright summer's day."

"This is too much for you," said the young man, seeing the woful tears gather in her eyes, her mouth twitch pitifully.

"No, no, let me go on; I am strong enough; I must tell you all—at least, as much as you ought to know—to justify what you had to bear. Long ago, Mr. Sargent, when I was little more than a baby, something dreadful happened at our house—all I remember of it was a little coffin covered with roses, carried by negroes down the avenue to our burial-ground—and after that, there were other baby funerals, and they were all blurred together in my mind. Until since I have known you, I never knew the real cause of my little brother's death—"

"Do not distress yourself by telling me

of what I have already heard," interposed Sargent, impetuously.

"You knew it, then? I suppose everybody did, but myself," she said. "But there is something at San Juan far worse — something no one knew excepting my poor, stricken mother who has carried the dead weight of it all these years, and our faithful Joshua who was in her confidence. After that terrible occurrence, my poor father became subject to fits of mania that took the turn of — of wishing to destroy me, also. To avoid parting with her husband whom she adored, and because in the intervals he was perfectly oblivious of his awful fancies while insane, my mother gave up her life to watching him and me. And to think she had no one to help her in her struggle, excepting Joshua, who would have died for her — poor Joshua, who *did* die for her!"

Her articulation was overpowered with tears. At the sight of her despair, Sargent sprang to his feet, and paced the floor, while the stolid woman at the wheel, aroused to notice what was passing, came over and stood behind the girl, and stroked her hair, with a grim attempt at comfort.

"That night," went on Ariana, finally, "he was excited more than usual by your presence and conversation. My mother, never suspecting the approach of one of his attacks, went away from her bedroom for a visit to my brother's grave, leaving, as she thought, Joshua sleeping as usual on a cot in my father's room. Joshua, who could not bear to have her go out at night alone, followed her, after locking my father in his room — it was Joshua whose hand turned the key on you, also, for your safety, Mr. Sargent; and it was I who left the note on your table when you were fast asleep —"

"Need you tell me the rest?" he asked, as her agitation began again to rise.

"Why not?" she said, with a dreary attempt at self-command. "I don't want you to think any worse of us than need be. My father awoke, found Joshua gone, and got hold of a key he had hidden in his last attack. He came into my room, and aroused me. For the first time, — God help me, — I saw him as he is.

The Secret of San Juan

Oh! it was too horrible. He told me he loved me so dearly, he had resolved to send me to stay with my little brother. I begged and pleaded — then I screamed for help; and after that — I believe I fainted. Mama came, and Joshua. Joshua captured him and carried him back into his room. When mama could leave me to go to them, she found papa quietly asleep, and Joshua sitting, dead of heart disease, beside his bed."

"And yet you sent me away from you?" protested Sargent.

"I did not know of Joshua's death till afterwards. Mama, who seemed to me suddenly the brave, strong, helpful person of the house, did everything. She made me write to you to go. Ah! Mr. Sargent, if I have lost one parent I have gained another — in all these years she has not dared show me her love for me, because it excited him. Her life has been one long sacrifice."

"These things are not for my ears," said Sargent, seeing what the recital cost her. "With all my soul I pity you. After this it will be impossible, for your mother's safety and yours, to allow Mr. Trevelyan to remain under the same roof with you. Surely you will let me act as I would for my own mother and sister under such circumstances."

"It is no use," she said. "My mother would not consent to part with him. It is I who am to be exiled. I am going away from San Juan to live with a cousin who knows our story. All I can ask of you, Mr. Sargent, who have been so strangely interwoven with our sorrow, is that you will forgive us and forget us. I know I have your sympathy. You saw how we loved each other. To spare my poor darling a knowledge of what he tried to do, I had rather go away from him forever—"

"That is, at all costs, your best plan," said Sargent, brightening. "And, by-and-by, when the memory of this terrible trial shall have worn away, will you allow me to come to you again?"

"I cannot tell," she said, listlessly. "I think I shall be better by myself. You see, Mr. Sargent, I am not as other girls are. Everything I love best is doomed.

The Secret of San Juan

Even poor Joshua could not be spared to protect me as he has done for years. For my sake he died at his post of duty. Yes, Mary," she continued, turning with signs to the mute woman who was following Ariana's agitated story with her eyes, "I'm telling about your dear brother, who was faithful unto death."

With a whimpering sound the woman shrunk away, resuming her seat at the distaff. To her, through habit, to Ariana who had wept so much, tears did not now come easily.

Sargent, after two turns over the cabin floor, came back to Ariana's side. "It is no use," he said; "whatever you may think, I can't help telling you. If you will give me the right, I'll devote my life to you."

"To me!" she exclaimed, turning pale and faltering. "To me?"

"What does anything matter, except that you are the one woman in the world for me!" he said impetuously.

"You forget that I am the last of the Trevelyans of San Juan," she said, color mounting into her wan face.

"I know what you mean, but since I laid eyes on you I have thought of nothing else but your loveliness. Your sorrows, the afflictions of your house, make you but dearer to me. Don't go to your cousin, Ariana; or, if you must, let it be for a time only; then come with me, as my wife, and in my love forget your past."

"I did not think there would be ever any one to say those words to me," she answered, still quietly, so quietly that his fire was, in spite of him, held in check. "You must be the most generous man in the world, Mr. Sargent; and indeed I'm not ungrateful. But even if I could love — if I could trust myself — I have made a promise to my mother — a solemn promise — never to marry any one —"

"No one has a right to bind you by such a promise — you, a mere child, with a lifetime before you!" he interrupted hotly, but, even as he looked, beheld in her face a likeness that made him stop suddenly and catch his breath.

"You see I am not like other girls," she repeated forlornly, finding no better phrase; and, after that, though their hearts were over full, conversation between them halted, until she bade him a sad farewell.

Sargent, after helping her into her canoe, stood on a gnarled knot over the water watching her light form till it was lost in the Stygian shadow of the swamp. Then, in a tumult of feeling, he embarked in his own canoe and pursued his way in the opposite direction.

Long years after these events, Sargent repeated his assay at voyaging along the Georgian coast. This time he was not alone, and, in the vigor of a successful manhood, and the fulness of a happy married life, he was able to revert with composure to the painful episode of his visit to San Juan. Through inquiry of old Adams, who was still pursuing his avocation of pilot for pleasure parties from point to point along the coast, he learned all that was known to the public of the late owners of the island.

Mrs. Trevelyan, who had died of natural causes, was laid in the cemetery across the feet of the children she had lost; and, on the day following, her husband had been found dead by his own hand upon her grave. The young lady, who for years had been living with a relative in another part of the State, was said to have come back on one occasion to visit her birthplace; but this, Adams remarked, was hearsay, as nobody knew for certain anything subsequent to the death of Captain and Mrs. Trevelyan, except the burning down of the old house one windy night of autumn.

"And yet," said the old pilot, reflectively, after he had delivered his information, "seems to me Fishin' Dick said he thought he seen Miss Ariana a year or two back at the marsh-house; she was goin' off in a flat-boat poled by the last o' them Parsonses, a deef woman — twin o' Josh., Mr. Sargent, if you remember him. All the rest o' the Parsonses had died; and the deef woman kept house there by herself for a spell; that's certain. P'r'aps Miss Ariana came and got Mary to live with her somewheres. And I forgot to tell you, sir, Fishin' Dick said the lady was dressed up like one o' them nuns he seen onst at St. Augustine."

"The Stranger Within Thy Gate"

"The Stranger Within Thy Gate"

Part I

A WOMAN, neither young nor old, good-looking, well-dressed, of a poise of manner indicating that she was accustomed to take the lead of affairs in which she had part, sat in a luxurious morning-room, dictating to a stenographer answers to the pile of letters lying open upon her desk and held in place by a paperweight incrusted with gold and gems. Many of these letters were in the form of application for help to their writers. Some looked business-like, and were reminders of dates set for philanthropic meetings or associations for semi-political ends. Others were invitations to be present at discussions by women of a variety of subjects ranging from Colonial research to the green carnations of modern fiction, or the study of modern decadent dramatists. With each in turn Mrs. Ordway dealt in admirable fashion — considerately, unemotionally, showing both judgment and good sense. Little Miss Clinch, the stenographer, to whose hard lot it had previously fallen to serve at the chariot wheels of some fashionable philanthropists of a different stripe, felicitated herself upon being in Mrs. Ordway's employ. In a short time the formidable pile of documents was reduced by two-thirds. The tense look upon Mrs. Ordway's face relaxed. Business was over, and she was about to regain comparative freedom for another day.

"You did not decide whether you will take the chair at the Mission Meeting for the Protection of Girls in their Teens," suggested Miss Clinch, going back to a request tabled while under consideration.

"Let me see. Wednesday of next week at eleven. That crowds the Anti-suffrage Meeting at twelve, doesn't it? But I think I had better risk it, in view of the importance of what is proposed."

At this moment there was a tap upon the door.

"Come in," said Mrs. Ordway, with a tinge of impatience in her voice.

"I beg your pardon, madam," said a decent elderly woman, entering; "but we can do nothing at all with the new housemaid who came last week; and I think there's no use trying to keep her. I believe the girl isn't quite right, ma'am. All last night I heard her muttering and catching her breath like, in the little room next to mine. So, if you don't mind giving me the trifle of wages that's due her now, perhaps it would be better to let her go, without further trouble."

"How exceedingly tiresome!" cried the lady; "when you had just told me she did her work so well."

"I know it, ma'am. There hasn't been one of them we've had in a long time that was as quick and tidy. The way she did the bath-rooms was a pleasure to look into, let alone the pitchers and basins, that I've generally such a trouble to get them to clean properly. But I've always noticed, ma'am, that when they're right one way they're wrong another. My own opinion is the girl is out of her head somehow or other, and most of the servants agree with me. They're all for having her go."

"In that case," answered Mrs. Ordway, smiling, "the voice of the majority carries the day. Miss Clinch, please get out my wage book, and enter this payment of four dollars for a week's services to date to Ann — I forget her last name — yes, Ann Woods, housemaid. Here, Martha, is the money. Of course, she can't ask me for a reference; and I do hope you'll get her out of the house without a fuss."

"Never fear, ma'am; she's not one of the noisy kind; she seems dazed like. And I'm surprised at such an office as Mrs. Climer's sending her to you."

"Perhaps she drinks," said Mrs. Ordway, with a look of disgust. "I shall make it my business to stop in at Mrs. Climer's and tell her she ought to investigate this person's habits before introducing her into another respectable household. She is young, you said, Martha?"

"Yes, m'm; Ann can't be above seventeen, but she's tall and hearty for her age."

"Then next time we'll have none but a settled person. Oh, dear! between old cranks and young flibbertigibbets, one doesn't know what to choose. Really," she added to her secretary, as old Martha withdrew, "things have come to such a pass with the servant question now that I try to ignore their presence in my house. Old Martha and my butler and the kitchen-maid are rocks who stand by me; but the rest come and go until I am worn out with thinking of them. If they were not, the matter would fall over me like a pall every time I enter my own door."

"Then I am to accept for you the chairmanship of the Mission meeting?" resumed the methodical Miss Clinch, who, in so large a measure behind the scenes of her employers in general, was well accustomed to complaints like the foregoing.

"Yes; and, while we are about it, let us jot down the points that occur to me for my opening address. I will take them with me presently to the meeting of our

The Stranger Within Thy Gate"

"The Stranger Within Thy Gate"

Hospital Board, where I can consult Miss Cranmer, who has so much more experience with that class than I have, about what is best to say."

Miss Clinch obeyed; and, as was Mrs. Ordway's custom in composing her fluent and incisive addresses, that lady arose and walked back and forth in the warm, brilliant, homelike apartment, where a wood fire and flowers, books and easy chairs and choice pictures, contributed to the sense of delightful comfort.

Puzzling for a moment over an idea she had not yet disentangled from the gray matter of her brain, the mistress of all this luxury paused in the bay window looking down upon the street bounding one side of her handsome corner house. It was drizzling rain, and a raw east wind swept up from the river, sending into retreat all pedestrians not obliged to be abroad. At that moment she saw emerge from her own basement door the figure of a young woman, carrying beneath her arm a bundle wrapped up in newspaper. The person had no umbrella, and her only protectors from the wet were a smart, cheap straw hat and a thin and tawdry jacket of drab cloth.

"'Taken away,' as De Quincey eloquently says," repeated Miss Clinch, "'before injuries and cruelty have blotted out and transfigured her ingenuous nature, and while yet there is time for reform.'" She paused longer than usual for Mrs. Ordway to go on.

"I do believe that is Ann Woods," exclaimed the lady, with a regretful accent; "and she has no umbrella. Martha should have seen that she had one. The girl certainly seems to stagger. What a dreadful thing if she should be under the influence of liquor, and coming from this house!"

The writing was suspended, while Miss Clinch came also to the window; and together the two women watched their forlorn sister swaying uncertain on the curbstone of the street below. After a brief time of apparent indecision the girl started out, walking steadily enough, in the direction of a line of street cars close at hand. As the last flutter of the wanderer's garments disappeared from view, Mrs. Ord-

"The Stranger Within Thy Gate"

"*The Stranger Within Thy Gate*" way turned around shivering, and went over to put another stick of hickory upon the fire.

"Ugh! I am cold," she said, extending her palms to the leaping blaze that presently sprang up. "I wish Martha had not let Ann go without an umbrella. Of course, she has friends, and will go to them — they always do; and the money I paid her will keep her for a week, until she gets another place. Somehow or other, inefficient as they may be, those creatures invariably manage to get another place. It is we, the poor mistresses, whose homes are disrupted by their quarrels and want of conscience, who are the real objects of pity in these days."

Nevertheless, Mrs. Ordway, who possessed a somewhat vivid imagination, recurred oftener than once that day to the image stamped upon her mind of the girl, scarcely more than a child, who had been obliged to flee out of a comfortable home into the stony welcome of the streets. At the play that evening, when a great actress was winning tears for the mimic sorrows of the outcast she represented, Mrs. Ordway forgot the stage and the splendid pose of the despairing Magdalen who held it, to think again of that lithe, wavering form in the drab jacket and cheap straw hat, with the bundle wrapped in newspaper beneath her arm.

"The Stranger Within Thy Gate"

Early next day, still under the spur of this reminiscence, Mrs. Ordway drove to the intelligence office whence the girl had come to her, and interrogated the woman in charge concerning Ann Woods.

"Ann Woods? I am sorry she left you, m'm. No, she has not come in here to ask about another place yet; but I suppose she'll be along in a day or two. I can't say I knew the girl myself, m'm; but I knew of her. Her father and mother both died last year, and she's only begun to live out. A pretty girl — too pretty not to be in a good home, Mrs. Ordway; and a nice, pleasant manner, so far as I can see. Don't know how she came to act so queer in your house. Never heard any such complaint of her before; but I suppose some of the other help went against her grain, and she got kind o' nervous. They will sometimes, and then they're ashamed of it; and no doubt that's Ann's trouble. She's proud, and she wouldn't want to think a complaint had been made against her here. I told your butler that, when you sent him yesterday after a woman in Ann's place. If you don't like the new person I sent, Mrs. Ordway, there's another, a Swedish girl, I think will give you satisfaction."

"Don't speak of another change," said Mrs. Ordway, laughing, as she went out and threw herself, relieved, into her carriage.

Of course it was as Mrs. Climer said. Ann, nervous and hysterical, had escaped from notice temporarily. But in New York, for a good worker and nice-looking girl, was there anything easier than to get a place at excellent wages, where her employers would be only too solicitous to make her satisfied to stay? Lastly, Mrs. Ordway asked herself, dismissing Ann Woods for good and all from her overcrowded sympathies, had she ever interested herself thoroughly in the affairs of one of her household servants when real gratitude, or even appreciation, had been her reward? She was glad, in this case, to be spared the usual result!

Part II

MONTHS passed on, and still Mrs. Ordway pursued her work for her fellow-beings with the capacity and cool zest that often made her twice as useful in an emergency as a more emotional and softer-hearted woman could be in her place. Delighting in the acts of direction and control after her inborn inalienable nature, she knew not fatigue nor tarried by the way when there was a scheme to be carried out in the face of difficulty. Naturally, she was the pearl without price of all boards and committees fortunate enough to secure her, and the amount of solid accomplishment laid up to her credit in a given space of time was known only to Providence and Miss Clinch. But in the middle of this admirable career — early in the autumn following the incident just narrated — poignant grief laid hold of Mrs. Ordway's happy, prosperous life, and, like an axe at

"The Stranger Within Thy Gate"

"The Stranger Within Thy Gate"

the roots of a healthy forest tree, brought her crashing to the earth. Her daughter, a young girl just entering lovely womanhood, died, after a brief illness of diphtheria; and thenceforward there was no more heard of her for many a day in the world of gay society — of her, a woman who had been so long one of its most active members. And as it is not intended that we may come out of great sorrow quite the same as when we passed into it, Mrs. Ordway brought back with her to the consideration of everyday affairs a softer side toward the personality of the suffering, a greater interest in individual cases, for which she was now not only ready but eager to let slip into somebody else's hands the manœuvring of undertakings for relief of wrongdoing and poverty in the mass. Her great energy of character took her again, erelong, into several of the more needy of her old charities, but it was not as a director that she appeared. In her deep mourning robes, with her pale, unsmiling face, she would pass from hospital wards to slum visits, and spend hours upon missions in the heart of such distressful regions of the great city as rent her heart with self-reproach that she had known them only by hearsay until then.

One day the matron of a small downtown hospital Mrs. Ordway was in the habit of visiting — because she had found there a field for her labors uninvaded by those who had been her associates before — greeted her, upon arrival, with an excited face.

"We have an interesting case brought in this morning, madam," the woman said; "a very young girl. They sent for our ambulance to fetch her from the lodging house where she was found lying unconscious upon her bed. The doctors have been working at her for hours with a new respirator, and they're beginning at last to have hope they may bring her to. As I'm pretty busy just now in the baby ward, I thought maybe you mightn't mind being by this poor creature and saying a kind word to her when she can understand it."

"No, certainly not," answered Mrs. Ordway, preparing to hasten to the spot indicated. "What was the cause?"

"Opium, they say; suicide, most

"The Stranger Within Thy Gate"

likely," replied the matron, who had no time to spend in multiplying words.

Stretched on the narrow cot where they had put her, still surrounded by the doctors, the patient lay stark and numb awaiting the full return of the trembling vital spark.

"She'll do now, by George!" exclaimed the chief surgeon to his assistants, who drew back on either side of the bed. "Ah, Mrs. Ordway; glad to see you, madam. If you'd like to help, here's your chance, for our nurses are hard run this morning. Keep sponging her face and let her inhale this liquid now and then. There's a fellow waiting for us in the men's ward, but one of us will be back here presently to make sure. It would be a good thing for you to try to catch anything she may say to throw light upon her story."

"Where did you get her?"

"Called by the police to a so-called lodging house, with a woman in charge whose only concern was lest this girl should die on her hands. Woman said the girl had hired a furnished room there some weeks back, and was out of money. Had pawned all her clothes but the dress she has on, and was found this morning insensible on her bed. Our people had hardly got the patient out of the house to put her in the ambulance when the hag slammed the door after them and locked it. 'Tisn't often you see one of the class she represents as good-looking and refined as this poor thing. There, madam, for the present, I'll leave my patient in your care."

"The Stranger Within Thy Gate"

Lying still and white, her hair dropping in loose rings over the pillow, her dark lashes sweeping a wasted young cheek, the soft modelling of childhood still lingering around her mouth, the sufferer suggested to Mrs. Ordway something, she knew not what, that laid hold upon the watcher's memory with a sudden, unyielding grip.

Where under heaven could she have before encountered this poor sinner, whom it would have been almost more merciful to let lie in the gulf of everlasting sleep?

Little by little she retraced her recollections of the preceding year; then suspicion was aroused; then came swift certainty.

"The Stranger Within Thy Gate"

Sick at heart, she recognized her discharged servant, Ann Woods. With horrible precision of detail she recalled the manner of the girl's exit from her house — her own bored indifference about it; the pitiful swaying of the uncertain figure on the curbstone in the rain; her disappearance, alone, into the maze of the great city. And oh, what a black abyss it was that lay between the safe shelter of Mrs. Ordway's luxurious home and the haunt in which Ann had sought her death!

In ministrations to the now fully aroused patient the nurse tried to forget the stab of these poignant thoughts. Erelong she had the satisfaction of seeing a more human look come into the distraught eyes, an expression of release from pain around the lips.

"You feel better now, I'm sure?" asked the lady, softly.

"Oh yes, m'm; it's like heaven to what it was. God bless you for taking pity on me! It's the first I've had in many a day."

"It is the doctors to whom you owe

your life. I am only the nurse, and I want you to rest now, and try to get better, and not let anything trouble you. Whatever you have suffered, it's over now. We will take care of you, after this."

"The Stranger Within Thy Gate"

"Oh, the sweet words!" cried the girl, wildly. "And I that thought I was goin' to wake up in — Lady, is it me you are crying for? Don't cry; I'm not worth it. I'm no better than the dirt in the streets; and sure that's the way the old woman's been treating me since I hadn't the money to give her."

There was a brief silence. The listener could not have answered. The speaker waited to regain her strength.

"And me just eighteen to-morrow, lady . . . But I wasn't always bad. It ain't much more than a year since I was bad. Lucky my father and mother died before it. If they'd have lived, they'd have saved me, maybe. Once, not so long ago, I had the thought in my mind to go to the lady I was living out to service with, and tell her about my trouble. But she was a great lady, one of the big highflyers; an' I was only one of her under-servants she'd hardly looked at. Maybe, if I'd ha' told her then—"

"Good God!" came in a moan from Ann Woods' nurse. The patient, unheeding it, continued to doze and ramble. When the doctor returned he found Mrs. Ordway looking so pale and faint that he insisted upon her leaving the ward at once.

"The police have informed us," he said, accompanying her to the door, "that the girl was called Nan Woods. What her real name is, of course no one can say. Before her attempt to commit suicide to-day, she was reduced almost to starvation, and I have no doubt was cruelly treated by the woman with whom we found her. As I told you, her clothing consists of the single dress she has on now, and perhaps you would like to send her something in that line. For the present she is doing fairly well, but there is great weakness to overcome."

"I shall come back this afternoon with clothes for her," said Mrs. Ordway, in a voice she hardly recognized as her own.

"In the meantime, here is money. Let her want for nothing I can supply."

"Certainly, certainly," replied the doctor, helping his visitor into her carriage, in waiting in the narrow, grimy street. "But, if you will let me suggest, madam, you take these things too hard. When you have our experience now— Good morning, Mrs. Ordway."

As the carriage drove away, its solitary occupant burst into a passion of long-repressed weeping. All that she had done in public in the way of conscientious endeavor during her lifetime seemed as nothing beside this one thing left undone in the very sanctuary of her home. With a thrill of fear she wondered whether what had so recently and distressingly come as a visitation to herself had not been punishment meted out to her.

Later in the same day, her spirits renewed by a faint hope of reparation through plans she had already evolved for Ann's future welfare, Mrs. Ordway returned to the hospital. Reaching the women's ward, she saw that a screen had been drawn around Ann's bed, and with

"The Stranger Within Thy Gate"

"The Stranger Within Thy Gate" trembling limbs stood for a moment outside of it. At this moment the matron, with a grave face, came from behind the screen.

"Oh, Mrs. Ordway," she said. "I might have known you'd be back. You never forget us when we need you. But it's all over with Ann Woods. She died just now. And I really don't know as I could wish the poor thing to live, after what she's been telling me."

His Lordship

His Lordship

IN the morning-room of a house in Hill Street, London, S. W., a council of three had been for some time sitting over the affairs of young Humphrey Augustus William Frederic Dale, eighth earl of Teviot, known to his intimates as "Tev."

The dominant figure of the council was a lady, of aspect large, fair, and troubled. She wore her bonnet, and that fact, added to the general appearance of the house in a winter livery of brown hollands, suggested that the dowager countess of Teviot had come up to town for the day only.

Standing with his back to the fire was a gentleman advanced in years, spare, hook-nosed, courteous, well-dressed — evidently in ordinary times a delightful and lovable old boy — but at present abnormally out of humor. He was Colonel Kilgore, cousin on the father's side and late guardian of the young earl.

His Lordship

The third member of the inquisition revealed himself in look and manner so unmistakably the family solicitor that enlargement upon his appearance were needless. Mr. Cliff was a type of a class as unchanging and as solid in exterior as the Bank of England. But, in spite of his composed countenance, in all the years he had been bestowing advice upon the noble house of Teviot, he had never at heart felt more depressed than now.

"I really think, Adelbert," said Lady Teviot, addressing herself to the colonel, after an interval of uncomfortable silence between the three; "I really think you might give me your definite opinion about my poor, dear boy."

"God bless my soul, madam," answered the old gentleman, explosively, "do you want me to say that I think he is a very bad egg?"

The dowager shuddered, extending her right hand to ward off the unpleasant image.

"No, Adelbert," she answered, angelically; "I do not ask you to be vulgar, and to wound my feelings, already lacerated by misfortune. If my son has been imprudent—"

"Imprudent! Imprudent!" interrupted the colonel, shifting his position to walk up and down the hearth-rug like a lion in a cage. "He has wrecked his future and brought you to poverty, and made himself the talk of the kingdom by his monstrous follies. That much is indisputable. The question now is—what remains to be done with him, and with Belmore?"

"He might sell one or two of the pictures out of the gallery at Belmore—and I dare say the gold service would fetch a pretty penny," murmured Lady Teviot.

"Pooh! A mere drop in the bucket beside his debts, and what the place costs to keep up," replied the colonel.

"Then, it will be no doubt best to let Belmore to some of those rich Americans."

"I wish we could be so fortunate," said the colonel, dryly.

"And this house is sure to be taken for the season at a good price; but he must do over the drawing-rooms. As for me, I can get on at Cosycote; for the house is comfortable, if small. Or we might go to Alassio, where one lives for a mere trifle. If I could only induce Tev to go with me to Alassio, I would tell Jennings to begin packing at once, so that we might start this week. There is the little villa Lady Dorking had last year; if we could engage it, by wire, Jennings wouldn't mind hurrying, for once. In that delicious air of the Riviera, Tev's health might improve."

"It is not Tev's health that concerns me," remarked the heartless colonel. "He is strong enough to do more mischief in his day, and my advice to you is to keep him away from Alassio. It is quite too convenient to Monte Carlo. No, my dear Agnes, Cliff and I are fully agreed on one point. There will be no money to carry on Belmore a week longer at the present rate. You must dismiss the establishment, and remove to Cosycote, where, with the trifle of income you will have, you can live at least respectably."

"As to giving up Belmore, it is only what I should have done, had Tev married Gertrude; so I am prepared for that.

But I am awfully afraid, Adelbert, that *His* my poor boy will hardly be content at *Lordship* Cosycote."

"I presume not," said the colonel, a grim smile in the wrinkles around his eyes. "But I hardly think I would trouble myself, Agnes, with preparations for Lord Teviot's accommodations anywhere in England, just at present."

"Then what — what is there to do? You know Tev hates travel for travel's sake. But no doubt it would be better for him to go somewhere, out of this cruel, carping society of ours, which has no mercy on the indiscretions of a lad."

"Hum! Yet London can stand a fair share of 'indiscretions,'" said the colonel. "However, my dear lady, there's nothing to be gained by harping on the old string. If Lord Teviot does us the honor to keep his engagement to meet us here this morning, it is possible we may obtain from him some token of what are his own wishes in the matter."

"Oh, Tev wishes only to please me — and you —" murmured Lady Teviot, melting at thought of her son's submissive

His Lordship state of mind. "I sent you the beautiful letter he wrote me, Adelbert. I have not had such a letter from him since that time he was in trouble at Eton. A young man capable of writing such a letter as that, Colonel Kilgore, must not be judged by the laws that apply to mere commonplace people."

"Unfortunately, society at large is not prepared to segregate Lord Teviot from mere commonplace people; and his offences against it have been too numerous and flagrant to be overlooked. In plain words, Lady Teviot, your son is an outlaw in most of the houses he was born with the right to enter."

The dowager burst into tears. Mr. Cliff, not unaccustomed to scenes of this nature, and in the case of this especial client having been treated to them more than once, walked to the window and looked out, clearing his throat in a fashion that might mean anything.

"To tell you the truth, Adelbert," sobbed her ladyship, "Teviot has disappointed me in many ways, but in nothing more than in his conduct regarding his engagement. I had every hope from the project of his marriage with Gertrude Clair."

"Lord Brelincourt has forbidden Lord Teviot his house, madam," replied the colonel, briefly; "and Lady Gertrude would be a brave woman if she took Teviot now."

"There are others," went on Lady Teviot, dreadfully depressed, but making a forlorn attempt to nail her colors to the mast. "With our large connection, Teviot can certainly find somebody as good as Gertrude Clair, and with as good a fortune, too."

The colonel shrugged and made no answer.

"Then there is no help for it!" exclaimed Lady Teviot, between genuinely bitter sobs. "He must marry an American."

At the moment of this dramatic climax the door opened and Lord Teviot came into the room.

He was a handsome, boyish young fellow, with almost a feminine softness of feature, small of frame, Celtic of coloring,

His Lordship and pleasant of voice and manner. Certainly there was nothing about him to suggest the traditional black sheep. And his attire was carefully and elegantly adjusted to meet the " last cry " of the fashionable tailors.

" Good-morning, mummy, dear," he remarked, cheerfully, kissing her upon one of her delicately marked eyebrows. " Good-morning, colonel. Mornin', Cliff. Who's goin' to do it now ? "

" Do what, my son ? " answered the dowager, trying to maintain her dignity.

" Marry an American."

" Oh, Teviot, do not jest about this ! It is your only hope," exclaimed his mother, tearfully. " Colonel Kilgore and Mr. Cliff will tell you that you have reached the last extremity."

" They have been tellin' me that any time this half a dozen years," remarked his lordship, grinning, while the colonel and the lawyer looked things unutterable.

" The last extremity ! " reiterated her ladyship, who felt, poor woman, vaguely pleased to have acquired a phrase at once expressive and unanswerable.

His Lordship

A few days later a huge Cunard steamer ploughing westward through a rough autumnal sea carried among her first-class passengers that ornament of hereditary legislation in the kingdom that dispenses civilization to the world — the young Lord Teviot! His only acquaintance on board was his man-servant, a discreet Briton. But, as no sooner does one touch the quays at Liverpool on the sailing day of a crack boat bound for America than a distinct atmosphere of the States makes itself felt, Teviot began almost at once to be at home among his fellow-passengers. The greater number of them were in families, returning after a summer of travel in England and on the continent. Before they had anchored off Queenstown to take on the latest mails, our young lord was identified by several aspiring members of the new world's society. While he stood in a bored sort of way, watching the greedy gulls swarm in the wake of the ship and the gymnastics of the young ladies of Cork who had come out in their rowboats to dispose of merchandise aboard, he was touched on the arm and accosted by a

His Lordship stranger in a fur-lined coat. Teviot's attention was just then riveted by the spectacle of a "wild Irish girl" slipping recklessly down a line from the upper deck into her boat below, wherein a man lay napping in the morning sun. He was not disposed to give ear to the newcomer. But the stranger, waiting patiently, ended by offering his card, with the assurance that he and his family, who were aboard, would be most happy to do all in their power to secure the social enjoyment of Lord Teviot during his visit to the States.

My Lord Teviot, however, was not thus to be thrown away upon a chance acquaintance of shipboard. The steamer sailing from Southampton two days before his own had carried in its mail-bags a letter addressed by the countess dowager to an acquaintance she had made in the Riviera the year before — a Mrs. Harvey Wing, a lady of high fashion at Newport and in New York.

Mrs. Wing was, when the letter came to her, still at her house at Newport, although the season there had long since died a natural death. She was feeling very tired of everything, and uncertain what she should next "take up." The marriage of her daughter, some months before, to a man who had shown early in the action that he meant to keep his wife under his influence, had deprived Mrs. Wing of present companionship; for, in that respect, Mr. Wing, who spent his days as far as he could conveniently get away from Mrs. Wing, was not available. It was horribly dull at Newport, and yet she could not think of opening her house in town till the time of the Horse Show, still some weeks distant. The aspect of the sea and of nature in general under the autumnal skies did not exhilarate her. To enjoy the country at that season one must have plenty of work or cheerful company, or a light heart; and Mrs. Wing had none of these. She was, in fact, in that mental condition not classified by science, but in our latter days commonly occurrent among women of her class; Mrs. Wing was in want of an "object."

We may now take the privilege of reading, over her shoulder, the letter from Lady Teviot, that, as the perusal progressed, recalled animation long absent from its recipient's face.

Many women, on receiving each other's letters, skim over the earlier portions with an intuitive feeling that the most interesting part will be found, like the snake's rattle, at the finish. Having assured themselves on this point, they go back and imbibe at leisure the information or dissertations they have skipped.

Thus, Mrs. Harvey Wing, surprised at an epistle from Lady Teviot, by whom, although they had exchanged protestations of friendship in the south of France the year before, she had fancied herself forgotten, made scant work of the dowager's dull paragraphs about the times, the weather, the Premier, and her own health. The exact point at which Mrs. Wing's eyes began to take on a look of animation, was as follows:

"I suppose you remember me mentioning my son, although his engagements did not permit him to join me at Cannes. He is going out in the *Lucania* on Saturday to see America; and I have given him your address, which I found upon a card that I fortunately kept. I fancy there will be no *His Lordship* trouble in his finding you or your husband, who, you said, was always in the city when he was not on his yacht. Either one of you would do to put Teviot in the way of seeing things a bit; but I must beg you to recommend him to the less expensive hotels, as he is rather down on his luck just now, and he has not, like you Americans, money to throw away. I have several times thought of you, since Cannes, when I've met your country people abroad, squandering on all sides and ruining hotels and show places for us — I wonder why they can't find something to amuse them at home, without coming here in such troops.

"To return to Teviot; as you always seemed so obliging and are a mother yourself, I will tell you, in confidence, that it is very important for him to recoup his losses in some way; and if he should find a match suitable to him in America I have made up my mind to bear it, and to pray that, in the end, it may be sanctified to me. I remember, now, that we got your daughter's wedding

His Lordship cards; so, having just settled her, you will be in the way of knowing how these things are done in your society. I am going to ask you to have an eye upon my boy, and keep him from making any irremediable mistake. You know one can't always trust a young man's judgment to choose right, when there are a lot of pretty girls, such as I am told you have over there — though, for my taste, they are generally too pale, and decidedly forward and overdressed. It is quite impossible that he should marry any but one of your great fortunes; a little one would not be worth while; and I hope she will be healthy and presentable, and not talk through her nose. They would live chiefly here, at Belmore, which is one of the finest places in ——shire, and there is a house in Hill Street, and a castle in North Wales, and one or two little estates where he rarely goes. I am about removing from here to Cosycote — two hours out of town — and if you ever come to England, again, you must let me know that you are in town, and come out to take luncheon with me, some day.

Teviot, as you will see, is one of the handsomest young men of his set, and he has beautiful manners; and although he has given us a little anxiety by his wild ways lately, he is only a boy, after all. Then, too, he lost his poor father just as he was going into Eton; and his guardian has proved very exacting and uncongenial with him, so there is much excuse for Teviot. If he marries a decent girl,— your women are pretty generally straight, I find, except when they are very fast, and then they are quite too dreadful,— there is no reason why my son should not settle down, and reform altogether of his youthful indiscretions. I am writing at greater length than I intended, but the subject justifies me. It is really quite a comfort to think I am sending my dear lad out to one who might be his mother — for your daughter was nineteen last year, I think, and Teviot is but three and twenty. No doubt you will see him soon, and I will leave the rest to you. If there should come a time when you think I could do any good, I will not flinch. I will go to America myself."

His Lordship

Mrs. Wing drew a long breath, and let fall the sheet. To her cheek, for a moment, sprang the good red American blood of Bunker Hill.

"It's too late in the day to expect the British aristocrat to change her spots," she said, hotly. "But it will go hard with me if I can't pay that old thing off, for her impertinence. When I think how she used me and my carriage! Who wants her lordling, anyway? As if we hadn't enough of them sponging upon us—"

From anger she subsided into thought. Many ideas trooped through her head, many schemes were evolved, dismissed, recalled, readjusted, before she felt herself relieved by the sense of anticipated triumph. As for the conclusion at which she finally arrived, to disclose it will be the burden of this tale; but Mrs. Wing's wildest imaginings could not then have compassed the measure of her ultimate success in "getting even" with Lady Teviot.

A characteristic feature of the situation was that, at the close of her reverie, the wave of patriotic protest in the offended lady's breast had subsided, to give place to a complacent satisfaction in the prospect that, after all, everybody — or almost everybody — would envy her the position of bear-leader to a perfectly new young lord!

The first thing needful was to write a letter to her husband, bidding him seek Lord Teviot, and fetch him to Newport for a week.

"It is a good deal to do for any one," she thought, sitting down before a desk littered with silver-mounted frippery, "to write to Harvey. On second thoughts, I believe I can get it all into a telegram. Harvey will come, of course; he can't afford just now to decline an overture from me."

And Mr. Wing, reclaimed for the occasion, appeared duly in the unwonted capacity of master of his own house, bearing in his train Lord Teviot and my lord's valet, a dark, fateful personage, who might have been twin-brother of the Sphinx. Teviot, on his best behavior, appeared to

His Lordship unexpected advantage in the eyes of both host and hostess. He was natural, good humored, and decidedly pleasant company; bore himself without ostentation, and seemed always anxious to be rid of the state attending upon the handle to his name. On the whole, Mr. Wing felt that if there were a choice between the various youngsters who smoked his cigars, ate his *entrées*, and drank his wines, this Englishman was remunerative beyond the average.

But even such a consolation for the labor of enforced appearance as the head of his own large, expensive, and troublesome establishment, and for conjugal attentions expended during the period of three unbroken days, did not suffice for the restless Mr. Wing. On the morning of the fourth day of Lord Teviot's visit, he explained to his noble guest that he had been called back to town on business, but hoped Teviot wouldn't, on that account, hurry himself about leaving.

On this point Teviot, who in the course of his varied experience had learned to recognize a good thing when he saw it, was fully in accord with Mr. Wing. The ease, the luxury, the completeness of life in the beautiful home of the millionnaire—in spite of a lot of people asking one out to dinner ten days ahead—seemed a direct recompense bestowed on him by Fortune for his previous suffering at her hands. Mrs. Wing, a youngish, lively woman, who looked out for all his comforts and in whose company he needed not to trouble himself with mental effort, as she supplied all that sort of thing herself, was the entertainer best suited to his needs.

So Mr. Harvey Wing at once returned to New York, and Lord Teviot continued to while away the melancholy autumn days in great comfort at Newport.

Thus far his lordship had given no evidence of more than a vague general appreciation of the young women to whom Mrs. Wing had made him known. The society of the fair sex seemed to him, indeed, less enlivening than that of the men attracted into the radius of his distinguished presence. Nor had Mrs. Wing disturbed the serenity of his enjoyment by any hint as to the dowager's intentions for her wandering son. Like a clever creature,

His Lordship

as she was, Lord Teviot's hostess bided her time.

One afternoon while they were out driving in her victoria a gleam came into Mrs. Wing's eye as she saw approaching them two girls on horseback, attended by a groom. One of these maidens was possessed of a rare and obvious blonde beauty; the other, small, dark, piquant, shone like a ruby in juxtaposition to a pearl.

"By Jove! Who's that?" demanded Lord Teviot, sitting forward, as, in accompaniment to Mrs. Wing's salutation, he took off his hat.

"That! Which one?" asked Mrs. Wing, indifferently.

"The light one, I mean. She is the prettiest I've seen, by far. How is it we never set eyes on her before?"

"That is Miss Cassandra Meigs, of Chicago," said the lady, as if dismissing the subject.

"The name's a mouthful, but she's a stunner. Where has she kept herself since I came here?"

"They've been in Lenox for a week."

"She's a stunner — that light one," observed his lordship, in whom did not lie the gift of original expression. Mrs. Wing bestowed on him a transient inscrutable glance.

"Many people prefer her sister's looks, — the dark girl, you know, — Miss Olive Meigs," she said. "They are orphans, and have been spending the summer here in the Van Schoonhoven villa."

"What — alone?" asked his lordship, with a stare.

"No; duly chaperoned by a lady who has been presented at three courts. Theirs is a peculiar case, and the newspapers will never have done speculating as to which one is to get the plum."

"What plum?"

"A fortune of — for the sake of local color let us say — fabulous millions. It seems that their father, who died a few years since, was so afraid they would be married for their money, he left the most eccentric of wills. For all their present and possible needs, married or unmarried and until they shall be thirty years old, ample provision was made by a trust which gives them an income, but keeps the estate until that time undivided. But it's generally believed there is in existence a later will, which is not to be produced until they are both married."

"Oh, I say," remarked his lordship—

"And that later will," went on Mrs. Wing, seeing, without looking, sidewise, "disposes of nearly the whole estate to one daughter — leaving the other with but a pittance. The puzzle is that no one knows which of them is to be made rich by that later will."

"I say," repeated the earl, incredulously.

"This is everywhere believed. People are pretty equally divided as to the Miss Meigs' attractions; but the uncertainty as to their fortunes keeps their admirers agreeably on edge. Portia's caskets, and the rest of it."

"But isn't it rather rough," exclaimed Lord Teviot, who did not understand the last allusion in the least, "upon the girl who's to be left out in the cold?"

"She won't suffer from privation in any case; and the mysterious document is supposed to recommend her to the consideration of her sister. After all, it's no worse than your fashion in England, of bestowing a rich feast upon one child and cheeseparings upon the others. But, as the matter seems to interest you, suppose we look in at their house on our return. I dare say they wouldn't mind giving us a cup of tea. You will have a better opportunity then of contrasting Cassandra's fair beauty with Olive's brunette coloring. And your call would be such a gratification to the lady who has been presented at three courts."

"Now you're chaffing me," observed his lordship.

But he made no objection when, a half hour later, the horses' heads were turned in at the gates of the Van Schoonhoven villa.

A tall cathedral clock, standing sentinel at the foot of the stairs, boomed five as the little earl followed his leader into the hall of the Newport dwelling temporarily in the possession of the two Misses Meigs.

The servants had just lighted the lamps, revealing the medley of eastern draperies, foliage plants, tiger skins, Moorish pot-

His Lordship teries, Indian brass, and Sèvres vases, that with chairs and tables and gold-worked screens form the customary encumberment of the modern hall sitting-room.

There, kneeling before a fire of logs, Olive, in her riding habit, was in the act of feeding the blaze with bits of drift-wood that sent up swirls of blue and violet flame. Behind a tray just deposited by the footman, a lady in black crepon and jet was transferring little scoops of tea from a Queen Anne caddy to a well-scalded pot. Occupying, as if by right, the very centre of the rug, and commanding the first attention of the newcomers, the beautiful Cassandra stood warming her hands, chilled by a long ride in the autumn air.

Teviot, when after due introduction he stood beside her, did not reach more than to Miss Meigs' shoulder. Olive, who as they came in had sprung up in pretty and unaffected fashion, and was now seated with Mrs. Wing on a small couch with many pillows, was in size a better match for his lordship.

As Teviot now looked into the fair immobility of Cassandra's face, the charm of her beauty seemed in some way to elude him. He found his attention wandering to the staccato sentences, the bird-like chirpings, the trills of girlish laughter that issued from the nest of cushions shared between Mrs. Wing and Olive. In that portion of his anatomy that did duty for a heart, the little man even fancied an impulse to think it would be rather nice if Belmore House had a mistress who could laugh outright like Olive.

Teviot, aware of the necessity in his case, had up to this time been dallying with American opportunity. Heartily as he objected to the yoke of marriage, more heartily he felt the need of cash and consequence now lacking to his enjoyment of favorite haunts abroad. And at last he had made up his mind to show the daring accredited by history to some of his historic forefathers. He was determined not to go home from America without carrying, as a mask for his previous misconduct, a rich and pretty wife.

Cassandra, now confronting him, seemed all that could be desired. Her inanimate magnificence of contour and complexion assured him that a Lady Teviot, *née* Meigs, might take her place unchallenged among the previous beauties of his line. He could count upon a welcome to her from his mother and her friends. The display of her would serve to rehabilitate him in the eyes of all but unimportant critics. Had he been but reasonably sure she was the owner of the fortune, Teviot would have felt he was falling in love in the best old-fashioned way.

Olive, on the other hand, possessed for him little "face value." She was not only small and brown and slim of figure, she was distinctly mischief-loving and unconventional. Her eyes, when he had been presented to her, had surveyed him with a glance of indifference tinged with mockery. There was not much to be said for her on the score of manners. Yet, when she smiled, there was something that caused him to look again quickly.

Teviot was quite sure she thought nothing of his factitious advantages of name and title. He had an uncomfortable impression that between her and Mrs. Wing was passing some merriment relating unfavorably to himself. But, all the same, her voice and laugh and gesture possessed for him an attraction he had certainly not language at his command to define.

His Lordship

Other people came in, among them a young man or two, who gravitated naturally toward Olive, whilst Teviot and Cassandra were as naturally left together on the rug. When Miss Meigs finally moved, in a slow, majestic way, to take a chair, Teviot felt constrained to follow her. With his back turned to Olive, the young lord was now enabled to fix his distracted attention once more upon her sister. Then Cassandra's statuesque beauty, her soft gutturals of speech, her large, unsmiling eyes turned upon his, renewed in him the conviction that, all things else being equal, he need go no further to find his bride. The first impression of her beauty took new hold of him. His imagination, piqued by Mrs. Wing's story, conceived the idea that the general attitude of those present toward Cassandra was one of recognition of supremacy. Absurd to suppose that the elder sister would be passed by for a mere chit of a creature like that little laughing Olive.

His Lordship

When Mrs. Wing arose to withdraw Lord Teviot from the scene, he observed, standing behind Olive's chair, a young man who bore upon his artless countenance an expression denoting that he would not yield his place there unless compelled to do so by an armed force.

"You must come again to see us, Lord Teviot," said Olive, hospitably, as their English visitor stopped before her to say good-bye. "By-the-way, let me introduce to you our friend, Mr. Christopher Strong —Lord Teviot."

As the two men perfunctorily shook hands, upon his lordship's face there was no particular expression. One American, more or less, made so little difference to him.

Upon the countenance of Mr. Strong there was manifest an unmitigated scowl.

"There. You had to speak to him," Olive said, exultingly, when my lord had passed on. "But how rude you were to the pretty little boy!"

To explain this situation we shall have to confide to the reader what Olive's legal protectors and nearest of kin were as yet unaware of. Mr. Christopher Strong, a young professional man of New York, in Newport for a day only, had very recently succeeded in wringing from Miss Olive Meigs a conditional promise to marry him, if at the end of a reasonable time her present predilection for him should prove justified by mature acquaintance.

Strong, who against his own better judgment had laid his future at the feet of this little witch, had now just arrived from town to find installed as her visitor the notorious Lord Teviot, against whom he had lost no time in entering an honest protest. But Olive, wilful as she was innocent of mind, had refused to hear what she believed an outbreak of jealousy; and the result was her audacious forcing of Strong into an acquaintance with the object of his animosity.

"Very well," said the young man, controlling himself with an evident effort. "There are not many points I'd wish to make with you. But I ask you to trust my judgment that Lord Teviot is not fit for you to know."

"Prove it!" she said, in girl fashion;

and, when he did not answer, stamped her foot. Seeing that he had no idea of yielding his point, the rebellion of her nature against constraint led her to regret that she had ever dreamed of subjecting her will to his. "Understand that I take orders from no one," she said, hotly — "and that I shall know and associate with exactly whom I please."

"You are resolved?" he asked, growing white around the lips.

Olive nodded. What further might have occurred in their ill-timed conversation was arrested by the departure of the other guests and the appearance, at Olive's elbow, of her chaperon.

Mrs. Blight, an adept in the art of hastening the departure of long-staying young men, had only that morning bestowed upon the girl a polished screed against this very aggressive and unpromising Mr. Strong. At the first glimpse of the aspect of affairs between them now, she felt that her eloquence had not been thrown away.

Mr. Strong retired without the request to return for dinner, that, considering the shortness of his stay, he had hoped might have been extended to him. And Olive, without a word for anybody, ran up to her *His Lordship* room.

Mrs. Blight, a sister of the first wife of the late Mr. Meigs, had been invited, during the last illness of that eccentric gentleman, to occupy her present post. She was the childless widow of an expatriated anti-American, to whom had been allotted the felicitous award of dying upon English soil. Her sacrifice of returning to reside on her native continent was balanced by her liberal allowance from the trustees of the estate. She, more than any outsider, was credited with knowledge of facts about the supposed will which was to make one of her charges an heiress of enormous wealth and leave the other only a fairly well-dowered maiden. In consequence, Mrs. Blight's relation to society was in marked contrast to that of the ordinary paid chaperon.

Whatever her knowledge, Mrs. Blight kept it severely to herself. No one could say that she faced to the right-about for one

His Lordship more than the other of her girls. The most that could be alleged against her was that she disapproved of matrimony for the young, and thought Cassandra's manner was thrown away upon a republic.

The three ladies, dining together on the evening of Teviot's first call, fell into discussion of the earl. Mrs. Blight, in a flood of aristocratic reminiscence, gave the others the full history of his noble line, his brilliant position in the peerage, and the beauties of Belmore House and park (which, in company with her late husband, she had once visited in a fly from the neighboring village). On the subject of Lord Teviot's personal career, the chaperon was less expansive, for it had now been some years since she had lived abroad: in any case, even the vices of the aristocracy were viewed by her through a veil of rose-color.

"Do you not think, my dears," she concluded, as they rose to return to the drawing-room, "that the young man has an extraordinary look of—ahem—race?"

"I think he is very nice," said Cassandra, placidly. "If he can find a mount, he is going to ride with me to-morrow."

"Contrast him, for example," pursued Mrs. Blight, not looking toward Olive, who, with two red spots in her cheeks, had been eating her dinner in silence, "with that specimen of the average American roturier — Mr. Christopher Strong."

"You needn't bother about Mr. Strong," said Olive, brusquely. "He's gone, and we sha'n't see him any more. I've made up my mind to cultivate his lordship. Just now Cassy has first chance, but if she'll give me leave I'll enter the lists with her and tilt for a coronet. It will be fun, for Mrs. Wing confessed that she has told him the old story about our financial prospects."

"The truth of which, my dears, you were only permitted to know last week, when Olive reached her majority," interrupted Mrs. Blight, elegantly, and was just then called away to write one of her model notes.

"And a great relief it was to have our minds set at rest on that score," said Olive, when the sisters were alone. "Now, Cassy, I'm badly in need of fun, but I won't go in for Lord Teviot if you say you want him 'for keeps.'"

"Absurd, Olive. As I said before, he is very nice, but I met him only this afternoon. I meant to ask you who you thought made that wrap Mrs. Wing wore to-day?"

"I don't know," replied Olive, absently. She was revolving schemes by which she might relieve her overburdened heart, punish Strong for having been true to her and to himself, dispose of Lord Teviot as an intruder, and at the same time still the pricks of her own conscience.

One day in December the young Lord Teviot set out from his lodgings near Fifth Avenue — Mrs. Wing had taken heed of the dowager's instructions to recommend him to a cheap abiding-place where he was at little expense for meals — for a walk in Central Park.

It was an unusually mild day, although ice held the ponds and snow lay under trees that, when the sun shone bright, stained the whiteness at their feet with purple isles of shadow. After coquetting for a while, the sun had gone altogether into seclusion, leaving the great city's pleasure-ground enveloped in pearly mist, through which the sounds of far-off fog-horns on the river, the whiz of elevated trains, and vehicles rumbling along the adjacent streets, fell deadened upon the ear. A lover of nature's moods might have found especial charm in the eerie look of the gray-green landscape, in the wood-smells called forth by dampness, in the promise of spring that thus insinuated itself amid the assertions of rude winter. But Teviot had for such things neither sight nor hearing. Perhaps, for the first time in his life, the little lord was possessed by a distinctly keen sensation of anxiety. Hurrying through the frequented portions of the park, he reached a certain bosky dell, its branches alive with gray squirrels and chattering sparrows, and disappeared within its precinct.

Since the first meeting at Newport of his lordship with the Misses Meigs, hardly a day had passed that he had not recklessly exposed himself to the influence of their society. In vain had been marshalled before him — at the Horse Show, the Por-

His Lordship trait Show, the Opera House, everywhere — a glittering phalanx of maids and matrons illustrating American charm and beauty. To all other women save the two fair sisters from Chicago, who were known to be handicapped by the terms of an exasperating will — and no one knew which of them Teviot preferred — he was as adamant. And as attentions to girls under their circumstances were as good as disinterested, some people even began to look on Teviot as that *rara avis* among visiting Englishmen — a man who was marrying for love.

To prove, however, that he had not altogether forsworn his nationality, his lordship accepted on all sides, and with no discrimination as to the givers, invitations to clubs, coaches, yachts, dinners, luncheons, suppers, hunts and visits out-of-town. The inconvenience of a future call to repay these civilities in kind upon his own soil was the less feared, because of Teviot's long practice in the matter of contracting debts he had no intention of ever being able to liquidate.

It was a pleasant life, and soothing to

one who had for some time seen nothing but the cold shoulders of respectable people in his own country, to be caught to the bosom, as it were, of select American hospitality, to be told off, in every company, to the society of the most dignified matron or the choicest young girl; to have precedence, everywhere, over the white-haired and reverend seigniors of the republican *beau monde*. Teviot, who cared little for his rank and less for his title, was actually puzzled to understand the extent of his own deserving in the minds of these patriotic Americans. But being a man, and a young one, he thought it all very jolly, and certainly an immense improvement upon what he would just now have been enjoying in his native island.

In the merry-go-round of dining and wining and junketing with his New York admirers, however, Teviot had not lost sight of the main chance. New York, for an episode, was pretty fair; and the Yankees on their own ground were a "good sort," certainly. But London, and Belmore, and rehabilitation of his bank account, were the objects to be striven for.

His Lordship Save for his entanglement with the Misses Meigs, immediately upon arrival, he might even now have had a mind at rest, with the certainty of fetching his own price in the matrimonial market of America.

It sometimes occurred to him to wonder whether there had been any mischief in the intentions of his first patroness in so soon running his bark upon the shoals. But Mrs. Wing, after her return to town for the winter, was so fully occupied with her own infelicities with Mr. Wing, that Lord Teviot had no opportunity to call her to account. The fact was that, though he admired the elder of the two sisters more than any other woman he had seen, and was fully persuaded she would fill all personal requirements likely to be made upon his countess, his vagrant fancy had actually attached itself with enthusiasm to Olive.

Never had Teviot experienced, at the hands of any woman, so complete a mental and moral overhauling as that bestowed upon him by this young girl. At no moment, since their acquaintance set in, had he been able to decide whether she was in jest or earnest. Her purity of mind, her downright speech, her wit and merriment, *His Lordship* were a revelation to the jaded little lord. In her company, he was continually undecided whether to enjoy himself, or to turn and go away in a pet. And although he could not but often suspect her inclination to afford him an opportunity to make love to her, somehow or other the opportunity had never come.

Thus matters stood when, after they had been meeting in a general way for many days in New York, and Lord Teviot had begun to chafe under a sense that she was eluding a conversation alone with him, Olive had given him a hint of something better.

Only an off-hand hint, to be sure, that if he happened on such a day, at such an hour, to be strolling in a certain portion of the park — he might perchance find her there prepared to talk with him uninterrupted, upon subjects of importance to both of them.

As might have been expected, no sooner had Olive gone to this length, than the earl began to pull himself together, and wonder what the deuce the little girl was after. Racking his brain for an explanation of her overture, he jumped at the conclusion that, like most of the women he had known best, Olive was, after all, a self-seeker, and meant, if possible, to get ahead of her sister by bringing him to a prompt declaration and offer of his hand.

Yet here, trotting up and down an alley of the little wood she had indicated, her hands close in her muff under the frills of one of those fantastic capes that keep man at his proper distance, he found Miss Olive Meigs, looking not in the least sentimental, but rather equipped for business.

"Come on. Walk up and down, while we talk," she said, authoritatively. "It will keep us from taking cold."

"Is that what you brought me here to say?" he asked, taken aback and piqued.

"No.. I brought you here chiefly to see whether you would come," she answered, giving him a side glance and a smile of the variety he had found irresistible. "But — there were other reasons."

"By Jove, I believe you'd get me to go

anywhere, if you held up your little finger," he exclaimed, with abandonment of thought of consequences.

"Don't be too sure. But, since we have been together, I have at least kept you from stagnating, haven't I?"

Another one of those side glances, and it was all up with his little lordship.

"Well, rather," he said, throwing prudence to the winds. "You see, I never saw anything like you, before. And I'll give you my word you're the only woman that never bored me. I don't believe I could stand another woman, after you—"

"Stop," she interrupted. "You have some conscience, I hope, and you can't think it's fair to delude a poor little Choctaw savage with false hopes. A little more, and you'll be making me a proposal."

"Well, what if I did?" he said, staring.

"Only that I, too, have a conscience, and I don't want to let a trustful young man, so far from his home and friends, commit himself to me without knowing the real state of my affairs."

Affairs. Ominous word. It brought back to Teviot his debts and duns, and even a dim vision of his late guardian and the protesting Mr. Cliff. And it chilled his affection for both the Misses Meigs.

"Besides there is some one else to be taken into consideration; my poor sister——" she said with a choking voice.

She had turned away her head. Teviot thought she was about to cry. Was there no woman living who couldn't "have it out" with a fellow without a cry?

"Poor, dear Cassandra, to whom you have paid just exactly as much attention as you have to me. How will she bear it? Even the newspapers are saying she will be Lady Teviot. Pray, don't speak till you've heard what I think it my duty to tell you now. Everybody knows over here how important it is for Lord Teviot to marry a great fortune, and everybody knows it's only for him to choose which one he will take."

"Yes," said his lordship, simply, as she paused for him to speak.

"Then I want to prove to you that, for your sake and for my sister's, I can be magnanimous. I want you to know that, only the week before we met you, Cassy and I were informed by Mrs. Blight that *His Lordship* by the terms of my father's will—" At this point the young lady executed a tiny, delicate sneeze, and the delay it occasioned was, to her hearer, the torment of Tantalus.

"Oh! good gracious, I just knew we should take cold in this damp place. Let us walk out to the driveway yonder," she said in a prosaic way. "Where was I? — oh, it's an old story now; we have known it for several weeks; there actually was such a will as has been talked about (my poor, dear father, how anxious he was to save us from fortune-hunters, wasn't he?)— a will leaving his whole large estate to one of us, and a mere trifle of income to the other — and the lucky one, as might have been supposed, was his eldest child, Cassandra."

Lord Teviot fairly gasped. For some moments he said not a word, then asked permission to light a cigarette. So absorbed was he in this occupation and in reassembling his forces to take up conversation at the embarrassing point where she had let it drop that he did

His Lordship not observe, standing under a tree on the western driveway where they issued from the wood, the figure of a very impatient young man, who looked much out of humor with the part assigned to him to play.

"You — you — a — surprise me — really," observed his lordship, when he could no longer keep her waiting for an answer. Internally, he was wondering how soon he could count upon finding Cassandra at home to him, and thinking with fine sympathy that one day he would make up her loss somehow to this very plucky little Olive.

"That is just where we differ," said Olive, in clear tones, as she beckoned to her side her waiting cavalier. "For you do not surprise me in the least. Mr. Strong, here, will bear me witness that I told him, not half an hour since, exactly how our interview would end. And, I am bound to say, he scolded me ferociously because I would carry out my plan."

Lord Teviot, perplexed and suspicious, looked from her to the darkling Strong.

"Don't speak to each other, please,"

said Olive, laughing. "This is my chance; no one shall take it from me. I told my sister also, Lord Teviot, of the lesson I meant to give you, and I had her leave to try it, though I have no idea that it will do you any good. Cassy shall know how nearly your heart has been in my keeping to-day, and I don't think it will help you with her. In any case, you ought to be told of two things more. First, that I'm engaged to marry Mr. Strong — please, Christopher, do keep still, and don't ramp over the road like that, I'm coming now, this minute — and, second — "

"I think I have had enough," said his lordship, with some semblance of dignity.

"Perhaps; but it is due to tell you this. My father, at Mrs. Blight's solicitation, made a will later than the one I spoke of, and by that Cassy and I — though we were not to know of it till I had reached the discreet age of twenty-one — share his fortune, equally."

"You will allow me to wish you a good-morning," remarked the little earl; and turning on his heel, he walked rapidly away.

[*347*]

His Lordship

It was a full year from that date when Lord Teviot returned to England. Before leaving America, which he had seen under many phases, he heard of the marriage of the younger Miss Meigs to Mr. Christopher Strong; and of the reputed engagement of her sister to a senator in Washington, who, to the gratification of Mrs. Blight, might be looked on by the American people as reasonably sure to represent them one day as ambassador at an important foreign court.

On the steamer going home, Teviot talked these things over with his wife. But they gave him less concern than did the immediate consideration of how he should present this lady to the countess dowager. There could be no cordiality between them on the ground of old acquaintance, since the new Lady Teviot was none other than the late Mrs. Harvey Wing, who had obtained her divorce from Mr. Wing some months before it occurred to her to enliven her wealthy solitude by again taking up his lordship as "an object."

www.ingramcontent.com/pod-product-compliance
Lightning Source LLC
Chambersburg PA
CBHW030302240426
43673CB00040B/1034